HAPPY GUT COOKBOOK

STERLING EPICURE
New York

An Imprint of Sterling Publishing Co.,
1166 Avenue of the Americas
New York, NY 10036

Copyright © Elwin Street Productions Limited 2017.
Conceived and produced by Elwin Street Productions Limited
14 Clerkenwell Green, London EC1R 0DP
www.elwinstreet.com

ISBN 978-1-4549-2852-2

Photography by Christin Eide, except Alamy Stock Photo: 19; Shutterstock pp3, 4, 5, 9,
10, 18, 21, 22, 25, 28, 30, 32, 35, 37, 38, 40, 42, 44, 46, 48, 49, 50, 53, 54, 56, 58, 60, 63, 65,
66, 68, 70, 73, 74, 76, 78, 80, 82, 83, 84, 87, 88, 90, 92, 94, 97, 98, 100, 106, 111, 114, 116,
119, 124, 126, 132, 134, 136, 138, 139, 140, 142, 144,.150, 152, 153, 154, 158, 160, 162,
163, 164, 165, 171, 172.

Distributed in Canada by Sterling Publishing Co., Inc.
c/o Canadian Manda Group, 664 Annette Street
Toronto, Ontario, Canada M6S 2C8

For information about custom editions, special sales, and premium and corporate
purchases, please contact Sterling Special Sales at 800-805-5489 or specialsales@
sterlingpublishing.com.

Manufactured in China

2 4 6 8 10 9 7 5 3 1

sterlingpublishing.com

HAPPY GUT COOKBOOK

GOOD FOOD FOR SENSITIVE STOMACHS

Cecilie Hauge Ågotnes

STERLING EPICURE
New York

CONTENTS

MAIN MEALS   100

SWEETS   124

SAUCES & SEASONINGS   150

CECILIE'S STORY

I have always had stomach problems, and ten years ago, after being thoroughly examined by a specialist, I was diagnosed with IBS, or Irritable Bowel Syndrome. At the time I was relieved that there wasn't something more seriously wrong with me, and I thought that I could learn to live with my stomach as best I could.

IBS is the standard diagnosis for patients with unidentifiable stomach problems, those who have been through all the usual examinations of their digestive system without any particular disease being discovered. The patient is declared unwell, as it is apparent something is wrong, but as doctors cannot find any other disease, IBS is diagnosed.

In the fall of 2013, I gradually became worse and by December that same year, I could not eat anything without getting terrible stomach cramps and diarrhea. I lost about 12 pounds in a few weeks, and out of pure desperation I decided to test the Low FODMAP Diet. This diet was developed in 1999 at Monash University, in Australia, by Dr. Sue Shepherd, and today the diet is recommended by gastrointestinal specialists in many countries, including my native Norway.

I eventually learned a lot about the kinds of foods I could eat, but it was not easy to find recipes. Because I had always enjoyed cooking, I took on my new food regime as a challenge, and began experimenting with low FODMAP foods. The recipes in this book have evolved after much trial and error, many profanities, and a few frankly inedible dishes. Fortunately, I am as stubborn as a mule, and now my family enjoys my healthy and delicious low FODMAP foods every day.

After a while, I noticed I wasn't the only one who wanted recipes for simple things such as sauces, desserts, and food substitutes, and so I started my blog, www. lavfodmap.no. The feedback has been incredibly positive. The recipes may seem plain to some, but many say that they like the way I share my experiences, both when it comes to my diet, and when I'm describing what it's like to have IBS.

Since I am neither a doctor nor a nutritionist, I will only describe the diet in broad terms. The practical approach is based on my own experiences together with experiences from the readers of my blog and patients I met while giving talks in Norway.

INTRODUCTION TO FODMAP

WHAT IS IRRITABLE BOWEL SYNDROME?

Irritable bowel syndrome (IBS) is a generic term for ailments that occur in the stomach and intestine, which are not due to any other disease. They are the most common kind of problems people have with their stomach/digestive systems, and it is estimated that as many as 10–20 percent of the worldwide population are afflicted with IBS. The condition is troublesome, but not dangerous. Common symptoms are:

- Bloating and abdominal pain that disappears after a bowel movement or release of gas
- Intestinal gas, rumbling, and bloating
- Diarrhea or a sudden urge to defecate
- Constipation
- Mucus in the stool
- Incomplete emptying

IBS is something that plagues many of us in varying degrees, but the causes of these symptoms are often hard to find. If you frequently experience one or more of these symptoms, and have not been diagnosed with another illness, you most likely have some level of IBS.

Although there is currently no cure for IBS, it is well documented that one of the main causes can be undigested carbohydrates. Symptoms, such as those listed above, occur when undigested carbs travel down the large intestine. We are able to handle this just fine in small amounts, but when that amount becomes too great, we may experience problems, which will be perceived differently from person to person. The best thing you can do is to learn how to live with the condition and to make changes to your lifestyle and diet that will help to ease the symptoms.

PSYCHOLOGICAL OR PHYSICAL?

Although IBS is one of the most common gastrointestinal ailments, we do not know exactly what causes it. Some people have long believed that the condition is psychosomatic; that it is a psychological problem with a real physical impact on the body. Indeed, many studies have shown that those who have IBS often also have psychological problems like anxiety and depression, and other indeterminate symptoms such as fatigue and joint pain.

However, according to Professor Trygve Hausken, a researcher on IBS-related issues at Haukeland University Hospital in Bergen, IBS is a very real physical condition, and many people actually develop psychological problems as a result of their stomach issues.

Women are also affected by IBS far more frequently than men. The advice from the medical field is usually along the lines of "unwind, try to live a normal life, and follow a healthy diet." However, everyone with IBS is not equally sick and symptoms vary widely from person to person. At one end of the scale are those who do not define themselves as sick, who are only occasionally bothered by symptoms, and who don't really care that their stomach has a life of its own once in a while. At the other end, there are those who go to the bathroom 15–20 times a day, or those who have not gone for two weeks. There are some who are plagued by nausea every day and feel sick pretty much all the time. Many in this latter group often have additional diagnoses like ME, fibromyalgia, chronic migraines, or other chronic diseases.

Most of us, from time to time, have had both diarrhea and intestinal gas without being or feeling sick. It is painful and annoying, however, to have intestinal gas, and it is uncomfortable to feel that you have to let the gas out a little bit at a time. There is a reason why babies can cry for hours on end when they have colic!

Very many people feel alone with their stomach problems. Few people talk about their digestion, and many women find it embarrassing to have a bloated stomach and to look pregnant without being so. It is annoying when your stomach sounds like it contains a tiny orchestra, and you suddenly have to run to the bathroom. On top of this, many people dread the demeaning examinations they may have to endure if they seek out a doctor. As with most people who define themselves as sick, they are plagued with uncertainty about the future. For example, they may be afraid that they will never find a partner, and those who have one may be terrified that he or she will disappear. It doesn't help to worry about such things, but it is very hard to just let them be!

Unfortunately, many people with IBS isolate themselves from social activities. Having diarrhea and intestinal gas can make being with other people exhausting. No one wants to socialize when they have to keep running to the bathroom, right? Stomach pain is uncomfortable, and when your stomach is bloated and tender, it can be hard to find clothes that fit.

If this sounds like you, then you are not alone! I highly recommend that you seek help and advice, either from a good friend, a psychologist, or, if you just need someone to talk to, from some of the many online forums. On Facebook, there are closed groups (so your friends won't be able to see what you've posted unless they themselves are a member), and for many people it can be a great help to talk to others in the same situation. On these forums you will find people who have followed a low FODMAP diet for a long time. You can ask and get advice about the diet, but also on IBS medications, medical examinations, and generally dealing with the condition. For many, it is a relief just knowing that they are not alone!

WHAT IS FODMAP?

FODMAP stands for Fermentable, Oligosaccharides, Disaccharides, Monosaccharides And Polyols and is a generic term for carbohydrates in food that are difficult to digest. What these carbohydrates have in common is that the small intestine is unable to break down and absorb them completely, so that a large portion stays in the large intestine. When the undigested carbs arrive in the large intestine, they absorb fluid and cause fermentation. This fermentation creates problems with gas formation, bloating, diarrhea, and/or constipation. This occurs in everyone to some degree, but people with IBS are much more sensitive to this gas formation, and experience increased discomfort when it expands within the digestive tract.

The Low FODMAP Diet was developed at Monash University in Australia by Dr. Sue Shepherd in 1999. Researchers believed that a diet with lower levels of complex carbs could help those with IBS. In April 2013, Shepherd and her colleagues published the results of a systematic review of all the research surrounding the Low FODMAP Diet, which concluded that a lot of data now points to a clear link between food and IBS symptoms, and that a diet low in complex carbs can relieve symptoms for the majority of patients. According to researchers at Monash University, 70 percent of those who suffer from IBS feel better when following a diet based on low FODMAP foods. The chart opposite details the basic food groups that are low in FODMAP and those that contain FODMAP to help you get started in identifying the foods that may cause your flare-ups.

WHEAT FLOUR AND GLUTEN

Because the Monash program recommends gluten-free, many people believe it is the gluten that is high FODMAP. This is incorrect. Gluten is a protein and, as explained earlier, FODMAP are carbohydrates. In wheat- and other gluten-containing flour varieties it is actually the fructanes that are high FODMAP. Gluten-free is recommended because the same flour types that contain gluten also contain fructanes: it's easier to stick with gluten-free than with "fructane-free"!

Also, remember that unless you have celiac disease, a little wheat, such as that in sauces, will probably not have any adverse effect. There aren't many fructanes in wheat and, generally speaking, wheat does little damage in small portions. For example, one slice of bread is listed as low FODMAP on the Monash app!

The problem is that people often eat an enormous amount of wheat in a day. They may have a slice of bread for breakfast, pasta for dinner, and more bread as a snack during the day. This would quickly fill up the FODMAP bucket!

Oats

Many swear by gluten-free oatmeal. However, it is completely unnecessary to choose gluten-free rather than regular oatmeal, unless you have celiac disease. Oats have few fructanes, which is what you are looking for on a low FODMAP diet. On Monash, $\frac{1}{2}$ cup of oats are listed as low FODMAP.

Spelt

Spelt contains fewer fructanes than wheat, but is nonetheless not fructane-free. It has been shown that some people can tolerate spelt better than wheat, so just try this out. I chose not to eat spelt during the elimination period, but I then reintroduced it later.

Note: A sourdough spelt loaf will be the best option, due to the fermentation process, which breaks down the fructanes.

A PRACTICAL APPROACH

I began following a low FODMAP diet in December 2013. For the first few weeks my symptoms just became worse and worse, and I was on the verge of giving up. Fortunately, I found by chance that I couldn't tolerate cornstarch, even though it is low in FODMAP. I experimented by eating two types of cookies: one with and one without cornstarch. The days I ate the cookies with cornstarch, I became worse, while on the days I ate the other type of cookies, my stomach was much better.

Once I had discovered that cornstarch was one of my worst enemies, my stomach gradually improved. I was less troubled by diarrhea and I had less intestinal gas. When you decide to begin a low FODMAP diet, it is important that you remember that there is no one way to do it. We are all different, and you will need to find out what your stomach likes/doesn't like, and what suits your routines. Some people will find it beneficial to be monitored by a nutritionist, who knows a lot about the diet, while others will get by just fine on their own. It depends on your ailments. Some people are noticeably better after reducing just a few FODMAP foods, while others must live on a restricted diet.

Eating FODMAP foods has a cumulative effect: I think being sensitive to FODMAP foods is rather like filling a bucket with FODMAP every time you eat. When the bucket is full, you feel awful. So, if you eat a little wheat flour one day, you might be fine. If, on another day, you eat both a little wheat flour and drink some milk, you might also be fine. But if you then also add in some apple slices, you may feel really sick. Whether you've reacted to the wheat flour, the milk, or the apple slices is hard to say. It could just as easily have been too much FODMAP on one day, or over several days, as it could have been a single food item.

As mentioned earlier, the point of the diet is to reduce or avoid eating foods with high FODMAP. I started by eating only "safe" foods. That meant low FODMAP foods that I knew I could tolerate well. For me (and many others), this was plain meat, fish, chicken, rice, potato, and egg. A lot of people can also eat gluten-free flour mixes, but please note that these contain several types of flour. If you are using these mixes, and you find that you still have stomach aches and diarrhea after following the strict elimination diet for several weeks, it can be difficult to pinpoint the specific problem ingredient. As previously mentioned, one of the major problems for me was cornstarch, yet it is low in FODMAP.

After five to six weeks, when I began to feel relatively well, I began reintroducing foods. I know that Sue Shepherd has a list of foods you should begin reintroducing (see box, below), but I thought that it would be a good idea to start with the foods I missed the most, and that's why I began with onion and garlic. For many people, the food item they miss the most is wheat flour, so they start with that before moving on to other foods in the same group (fructanes), such as onions and garlic. Because some foods contain several types of FODMAP (for example, apples contain both fructose and polyols), it is not a good idea to start with these. Don't begin by eating large amounts of a particular food, but eat a little at a time and gradually increase your portions. For example, when it comes to wheat bread, start with perhaps a quarter of a slice a day over several days, and if you do not notice any reaction, increase this to half a slice per day. Continue until you are up to two slices.

On the days I have reintroduced foods, I make sure I only eat other foods I know I can tolerate so that I don't end up eating two "unsafe" foods. If I did, and I found I was having problems with my stomach, it would be difficult to know which food had caused the reaction.

Reintroducing foods can be a time-consuming process. You never have the time or the inclination to have a bad stomach! I know that there are many people who reintroduce foods on days when they know they don't have anything important to do. I try to do this, too. I also give in to temptation every now and then by eating foods that I know make me feel sick, but I only do this when I know I'm not going to be doing anything the following day, so that I can stay at home if I feel particularly unwell.

REINTRODUCING FOODS

Dr. Sue Shepherd, developer of the FODMAP diet, has a preferred order in which you should try reintroducing foods. Her reasoning is that many foods contain more than one FODMAP, and by testing foods in this order, you can avoid misinterpretations.

ORDER OF PRIORITY WHEN TESTING FOODS:

Polyols such as mushrooms, cauliflower, artificial sweeteners

Lactose (disaccharides) such as milk, yogurt, soft cheeses, goat milk cheese

Fructose (monosaccharides) such as mango, fresh figs, honey

Fructans (oligosaccharides) grains such as wheat, rye, barley, and onion, garlic

Galactans (oligosaccharides) such as beans, lentils, peas

EXAMPLES OF FODMAP IN THE MOST COMMON FOODS

Food Group	Low FODMAP (can be eaten)	FODMAP (should be limited)
Fruit	Blueberries, strawberries, grapes, kiwi, citrus fruits, raspberries, unripe bananas	Apples, pears, mango, canned fruits, watermelon, honey, dried fruits, fruit juices, fructose
Vegetables	Carrots, celery, green salads, spinach, olives, potatoes	Asparagus, broccoli, Brussels sprouts, beans, legumes, cabbage, fennel, garlic, onions, avocado
Grains/ cereals	Rice, oats, polenta, cornmeal, buckwheat, quinoa, gluten-free bread, pasta, and cereal products	Rye, barley, wheat
Dairy	Lactose-free milk, yogurt, cream, sour cream; rice milk; hard white cheeses; white mold cheeses (Brie, Camembert, etc.); lactose-free or rice-based ice cream	Milk, ice cream, cream, sour cream, goat cheese, and fresh and soft white cheeses
Sweeteners	Sugar, glucose, syrup, any sweetener that does not end in "-ol," including aspartame	Sorbitol, mannitol, isomalt, maltitol, xylitol, honey

Note: Meat, fish, eggs, and fat/oil do not contain FODMAP.

Inulins and FOS (fructooligosaccharides)/probiotics: These are water-soluble fibers that are basically good for the stomach, but still high in FODMAP, and many people react to them. They are found in products where the manufacturer increases the fiber content, for example in fruit yogurt or gluten-free products. In addition, FOS or inulin is often added to probiotic products (products with added lactic acid bacteria) and nutritional drinks.

LOW FODMAP FOODS

Many people will find that they can eat more varied foods, including using more fiber than I do, while some will have to be even more cautious. The recipes in the book are adapted to suit a delicate stomach, but if you can withstand more coarse-textured flour and vegetables, you can of course replace some of the flour with whole-grain flour and add in more vegetables that you can tolerate.

Flours

Many people with IBS may react to fiber. Even I get diarrhea from the smallest amount of fiber, so I therefore avoid using whole-grain, gluten-free flours, and instead stick to fine flour. Low FODMAP varieties are pre-made gluten-free mixes, potato flour, rice flour, cornstarch, cornmeal, sorghum, millet, buckwheat, and quinoa flour. Baking powder and baking soda are also safe to use.

Vegetables

Low FODMAP vegetables include spinach, tomato, carrot, cucumber, bell pepper, the green part of scallions, chives, and kale. Many people find it strange that vegetables such as red cabbage, broccoli, and rutabaga are also low FODMAP. Remember that many vegetables become high FODMAP if you exceed a certain amount. You should also not eat too many different vegetables at the same time, as you will quickly exceed the FODMAP limit. For many, the fiber in vegetables can be a problem, so take note that you may react to some vegetables, even though they are listed as low FODMAP. I can't tolerate, for example, cucumber and bell pepper.

Fruits and Berries

Low FODMAP fruits and berries include cantaloupe, grapes, orange, kiwi, pineapple, unripe banana, strawberry, blueberry, raspberry. The same rule applies here as for vegetables. A little bit is usually fine, but there is a limit to how much you should eat because many, including low FODMAP fruits, do contain fructose. To find your limit, you just have to test your way through. I would not recommend eating, for example, several oranges, kiwi fruit, pineapple slices, and strawberries in one day. This could be a disaster, and not only for IBS stomachs. The fiber in fruit can also irritate some IBS stomachs.

Milk Products

Low FODMAP milk products include all lactose-free dairy products, as well as hard cheeses and cottage cheese, which are naturally low in lactose. Some processed cheese spreads are also low in lactose. Remember that the majority of people, including those who are lactose intolerant, can actually cope with small amounts of lactose. Butter contains very little lactose and is tolerated by most people. As I'm a fan of using products that are easy to source in most supermarkets, I choose not to buy expensive lactose-free butter. This works fine for me, even though a blood test proved that I am lactose intolerant.

Sweeteners

Low FODMAP sweeteners include sugar, corn syrup, aspartame, and stevia but absolutely NOT honey or high fructose corn syrup, which are high FODMAP. Saccharin (or erythritol) has been much discussed and some believe it is fine to use (because the molecules are smaller than in other sugar alcohols and therefore contain virtually no carbs), while others do not. Since saccharin is apparently a borderline product, I would only try it out during reintroduction.

Many people think that sugar is high FODMAP, but it isn't. Sugar is made up of part glucose and part fructose, and most people tolerate eating sugar, albeit in limited quantities. You have to navigate your own way through, as some people tolerate sugar, while others do not. If you want to avoid sugar, replace it with a sweetener such as stevia. Since I tolerate sugar relatively well, I have little experience of using stevia in cooking. Stevia is quite similar to regular sugar in taste, but it can be difficult to substitute for sugar in recipes, because it is so much sweeter. You can find both recipes and advice on the internet, in books, and on the stevia packaging.

Note: Glucose helps in the digestion of fructose, so if a food contains more glucose than fructose, it will be low FODMAP. Foods with glucose-fructose syrup may, therefore, also be fine.

Herbs and Spices

Both fresh and dried herbs are low FODMAP. Since we cannot eat onions and garlic, I recommend using a lot of herbs to add flavor instead! My experience is that cayenne pepper and ginger are very good flavor substitutes for garlic. Even if they don't deliver the same taste, they do give the dish a "kick." Please note that some stomachs may react to strong spices such as chili and cayenne pepper. Work with your own tolerance and do not make your food too spicy if you know it irritates your stomach. Be careful of pre-made spice blends and any general ingredients listed as "spices" on labels, as these blends often contain onion and/or garlic.

Meat, Fish, and Eggs

These foods are all proteins, meaning you can eat virtually unlimited quantities. Just check that the meat/fish is not marinated in onion or garlic, and that pre-mixed products such as fish patties, sausage, and meatballs are onion- and garlic-free, dairy-free, and wheat-free.

Drinks

Low FODMAP drinks include water, lactose-free dairy products, filter coffee, fruit juice, and drinks that do not contain high FODMAP fruits and/or sweeteners ending in "-ol" (see chart on page 14). Alcohol is mostly low FODMAP, but watch out for sweet drinks like sherry or port, and carbonated mixers that may contain fructose. That said, there are many people who react to both carbonated drinks and alcohol.

Controversial Foods

Some foods remain controversial, with sources giving conflicting information (Monash says that only sourdough bread with spelt is low FODMAP, while other sources say that all spelt is low FODMAP). Monash says one thing, nutritionists say something else, and various websites will have their own theories. Even so, I mostly trust Monash; they have tested foods one by one in their lab. If I'm in doubt as to whether I will tolerate a food item, I test it out myself in small amounts to see if my stomach will react.

ONIONS AND GARLIC

Onions and garlic are some of the "worst culprits," and even healthy people who do not have stomach problems or IBS often react to them. You can eat the green part of scallions because the fructanes are located in the bulb and not in the green parts. Chives and the green parts of scallions are good flavor additives when you can't eat onions and garlic. Some people can, however, react to the green part too. It depends on how sensitive you are. It is therefore a good idea to try them out gradually!

Due to the fact that the fructanes in garlic are water soluble, garlic-infused oil is safe to use. You can either buy pre-made garlic-infused oil (the problem with this is that you cannot guarantee the quality), or you can make your own by chopping up garlic cloves, and then sautéing them in oil over medium heat for 4–5 minutes. Remove and discard the garlic, and use the oil in salads or for frying. By doing this, the fructanes do not end up in the oil, and the garlic will only add flavor.

Note: The oil must be used right away. It should not be stored, as this can allow bacteria to grow that can cause serious food poisoning. The safest course is to make the garlic-infused oil in a small pan just before you want to use it.

STAPLE FOODS

Here are some of the foods I always have in the house and use a lot:

- lactose-free milk
- lactose-free cream
- lactose-free sour cream
- butter
- eggs
- carrots
- scallions
- potatoes
- rice
- rice noodles
- olive oil, corn oil, sunflower oil
- salt
- pepper
- chili
- cayenne pepper
- dried and fresh herbs

- balsamic vinegar
- Kissan brand ketchup (available online) (other types can contain onion/garlic)
- soy sauce
- canned tomatoes
- rice flour
- gluten-free flour mix
- potato flour
- cornmeal
- 70% baking chocolate/lactose-free chocolate
- potato chips with salt (without onion powder)
- gluten-free pretzels (fantastic to keep in your bag)

THINGS TO WATCH OUT FOR

- Pre-made foods may contain onion or garlic powder, wheat flour, and lactose
- Gluten-free flour may contain pea flour or apple fiber
- Ham and cold cuts may contain onions and onion powder
- Jams and jellies can contain sweeteners ending in "-ol"
- Candy may contain artificial sweeteners ending in "-ol" (even if it is not labeled as sugar-free candy)
- Check ingredient labels for sweeteners/sugar alcohols, which end in "-ol," and are polyols: sorbitol, xylitol, maltitol, mannitol

FREQUENTLY ASKED QUESTIONS

HOW QUICKLY DOES THE DIET WORK?

My experience was that I got better quickly on a low FODMAP diet. The gas disappeared relatively quickly, and after just two to three days, I felt an improvement. When it came to the diarrhea and unstable defecation pattern, it took five to six weeks of following a strict low FODMAP diet, but some people may see an improvement a lot sooner. For those suffering from constipation, results may vary. Most people I know get rid of their intestinal gas problem on the diet, regardless of whether or not they are suffering from diarrhea or constipation!

If you have IBS, I would definitely recommend trying the diet for at least five to six weeks. It may be a good idea to consult a nutritionist for help. However, most people I know who go on the diet have read about it (via books and/or the internet), downloaded the Monash University app, and tried it on their own. Research shows that the diet helps 60–70 percent of those with IBS, and according to my doctor, this constitutes a very high success rate within the field of medicine.

I also know many people with Crohn's disease and ulcerative colitis who have felt better by following the diet, but there has not been a great deal of research into this. Sue Shepherd does, however, also recommend the diet to this patient group in her book. Since the Low FODMAP Diet is both gluten- and lactose-free, it can also suit those with celiac disease and lactose intolerance.

"The Low FODMAP Diet is not a quick fix," say nutritional physiologists. I agree with this to a certain extent. At the same time, I think that if you struggle with a lot of intestinal gas, it cannot hurt to follow low FODMAP principles a few days before, for example, attending a party where you would like to have a flat stomach for a party dress. You may find that you notice a difference after doing nothing more than just cutting out onion and garlic, which are the worst offenders, and limiting your intake of wheat for a few days.

HAVE I BEEN CURED BY THE LOW FODMAP DIET?

It depends on how you define "cured." My stomach will probably always react to foods with high FODMAP, but as long as I follow a low FODMAP diet, I am able to stay relatively symptom-free. I have much better control over my stomach than before I began the diet, which in turn makes me feel more in control in my everyday life, and gives me a greater sense of freedom. Thus, I can deal with occasionally having a few "bad stomach" days.

I have confidence in the research behind the Low FODMAP Diet and the knowledge of what food items with high FODMAP do inside the intestines, but I am also convinced that part of the reason the diet works is psychological. By going on a low FODMAP diet, you are actively doing something to get better, which is a way of taking control over your body. Your stomach no longer has a life of its own, and you are now making the decisions. For me, this was a big psychological relief.

On the other hand, "bad stomach" days can remind you that you are not totally in control, and when this happens, many people begin frantically searching for the reason their stomach has rebelled. All food intake over the last 48 hours is analyzed up and down, back and forth, and suddenly you begin to wonder if even "safe foods" could be the culprits. Here, I think it is important to take back control. Make a quick review of what you've eaten, and if you find nothing wrong, calm down and accept that it is completely normal to have the occasional bad day. Even those who do not have IBS have days when they feel awful, have diarrhea without any specific reason, or suffer from a lot of intestinal gas.

HOW DO I COPE WITH SOCIAL EVENTS?

I've taken two courses/seminars on IBS: one through the National Association Against Digestive Disorders (LMF) and one organized by the Haukeland Hospital in Bergen, Norway. Both courses had presentations by and with IBS patients. What struck me during both of these lectures was that the course participants were told to be better at saying "no," and to learn how to prioritize. In my experience, however, those of us with IBS actually say "no" far too often.

We don't avoid situations because we don't want to be sociable—we avoid them because we are genuinely sick and can't leave the bathroom, or because of the nagging fear that we are going to get sick. The former is, of course, a real problem. Sitting on the toilet means you're stuck, and there is very little you can do about it. Many of us have periods when we feel really well, but even then the anxiety that we might get sick is a nuisance. Not only do we have to say, "No, thank you" to a lot of invitations, when we are genuinely not feeling well, but in addition we cancel things we really want to do because we are afraid things will go badly. This doesn't leave much opportunity to be sociable and to enjoy ourselves, our friends, and our families.

My advice is to say "yes" a lot more often! It is better to go to an event and then go home if you end up feeling sick, than to decline and never know if you could have had a good time. In my experience, things are usually just fine!

That said, I think it is important to find a balance. There is no point in pushing yourself during bad times, when you are just depressed and tired, and when both your stomach and your anxiety take over. At that point, it's easy to end up in a downward spiral. Instead, just make sure that you use your good periods to make social calls, go out with friends, and take the initiative to do something. You may have to go home from some activities, but at least you tried! The good feeling you get when you accept invitations and end up having a great time is a real boost.

It can also be a good idea to find a hobby—something you are genuinely interested in and that you can develop. When you focus your thoughts on something else, and enjoy what you are doing, you'll feel great and know that you are coping well.

Another piece of advice is to be open about your stomach problems. It's good for your friends and family to know that when you decline invitations it's not because you don't want to attend, but because you simply cannot. Let those around you know when you are sick. If you disappear from a party and are gone for half an hour, they will know where you are, and when you reappear you won't have to explain. It is also good to laugh a bit about it, as humor is liberating and can break down taboos. When I am on a flight, I have often let the cabin crew know if I'm feeling sick. They might give me a little extra food, three seats together, or perhaps I might get to sit in the back, near the toilet. I always try to get an aisle seat near the toilet so that I can get to the bathroom without having to disturb others.

DO YOU HAVE TO BE SUPER HEALTHY TO FOLLOW THE LOW FODMAP DIET?

If you ask a nutritionist, you will probably get a different answer from the one I give. I am a fan of the "everything in moderation" principle. I have always been fond of food and good flavors, regardless of whether they are healthy or not. Fortunately, vegetables, fruits, and healthy foods are some of my favorites, but candy and treats are also my weaknesses. When I started on a low FODMAP diet, I was traveling and I would dutifully eat a plain piece of meat or fish with potatoes or rice, without sauce, for dinner. Then I would sit enviously and watch everyone else eat dessert. That's when I decided that I had to get home and explore how I could make really good low FODMAP food myself!

So yes, I often use cream and sour cream, as well as salt and sugar, to bring out the flavors in my food. Still, I think that I eat more diversely and more healthily in my everyday life now than I did before. Many temptations that were easy to give in to before, such as candy (a lot of candy contains sorbitol), pastries, chocolate, and cakes, are not now included in my daily diet, which makes me think that I deserve to enjoy a little cream and sour cream in my recipes, and a bit of low FODMAP cake or dessert on the weekends.

It has been important for me to be able to take some calculated risks, such as eating garlic, onion, or wheat, once in a while. But I make sure I wipe my calendar clean so that I am not busy over the next few days. The benefit of this is not just that I can sometimes give in to the temptation, but that—especially the next day—I am reminded why I no longer eat those foods regularly.

LIVING WITH THE LOW FODMAP DIET

When I'm at home, I feel very "free" with regard to food. I make a lot of good, low FODMAP meals, and I don't feel like I'm missing anything (except when I'm making cinnamon rolls for my husband and children). When I'm traveling, on the other hand, I notice that I quickly get tired of both my stomach and my limited diet. Imagine your dismay if you were staying at a nice hotel, and you had to ask for a few slices of plain ham and rice instead of the delectable dishes you could see everyone else enjoying. I try to tell myself that food does not have to be the focus when I'm traveling, and that I should just be happy that I am able to travel, but it is not always easy. It is particularly difficult when the travel party goes to an Italian or Indian restaurant, and I have to tell them nicely that I cannot eat anything on the menu. Just then, a low FODMAP diet feels like a straitjacket.

It is also easy to become obsessed with food and with monitoring any reactions you have to different ingredients. It sometimes feels as if I've jumped on a carousel that is going faster and faster, making me more and more dizzy and lightheaded, and I can't jump off. At this point, it's not easy to think straight!

When you follow a restrictive diet, such as a low FODMAP diet, it is important always to remember that if your stomach hurts, it isn't necessarily a specific food that is to blame. Sometimes it can be a random combination of food and how you feel that day, and at other times there may be other reasons. Even if IBS is not a psychological disorder, stress can exacerbate the condition. And sometimes stomach trouble is caused by something as annoying as a stomach virus or flu. It is important to keep in mind that it is not completely abnormal, even for people without IBS, for the stomach to be a bit unstable. After following the diet for almost one year, and being in contact with many others who also follow the diet, I have discovered that we share some common challenges: What do I eat for breakfast and lunch? What do I do in social situations? What do I do when eating out? At a lunch buffet, at work?

Since starting the diet, I've found it easier to stick to it if I put the emphasis on the social gathering, rather than on the food. It is much better to socialize with people and have a good time, even if it means eating just a piece of meat without the sauce, than to stay at home because I am afraid of getting sick from the food that might be served!

BREAKFAST, LUNCH, AND SNACKS

Many people struggle with breakfast and lunch. It has a lot to do with the fact that we are used to eating bread at these meals, and when we begin a low FODMAP diet, we become a bit too focused on everything we cannot eat. Many people are afraid that their diet will become too monotonous. I felt the same way, until I started thinking about what I used to eat before I started a FODMAP diet. My diet was actually much more monotonous than it is now! Most people eat cereal for breakfast and sandwiches for lunch, day after day. If you want to, you can continue with this routine, but you will need to make your toast and sandwiches with gluten-free bread. Here are some alternative suggestions, however, for some variety:

Breakfast: Fried or boiled eggs, or omelet (see page 44) with a little ham and/or fried potato. Rice cakes, gluten-free scones (see page 32), focaccia (see page 92), waffles (see page 74), pancakes (see page 38), or choux pastry (see page 70) with toppings such as hard cheeses, ham, eggs, tuna, peanut butter, half a banana, cottage cheese, or low FODMAP jam.

Lunch: Stir-fried rice with low FODMAP vegetables and a little meat or fish. Any leftovers from the main meal recipes in this book are great the next day, as are savory muffins (see page 94) with a low FODMAP filling/topping of your choice.

EATING OUT

I know that many people, when eating out, will contact the restaurant in advance. They explain what they can or cannot tolerate and ask for a special dish to be made. This is a good idea if you are going to a fine-dining establishment, but for me it is too much effort to call every time I eat out. I did, however, do this when my husband and I were celebrating our birthdays and had booked an especially nice restaurant. To my great joy (and surprise), the chef had taken the time to read about the diet so that he could make a low FODMAP meal for me.

I have learned that it is easier to say what I can eat, instead of listing everything I can't. It will quickly become very confusing for the poor person who takes the message, and

you may still end up with food you can't eat. Therefore, I often ask just for plain broiled meat or fish with salt and pepper.

If you have a lunch buffet at work, the catering staff should be able to help you make sure there are foods that you can eat, such as broiled meat, fish, seafood, potatoes, rice, eggs, salads, etc. If they do not have gluten-free crackers or bread, you can always bring those with you. Most buffets at hotels and restaurants have some low FODMAP food options. See the list on page 14, and choose the foods that you know work for you.

If you have a refrigerator at work, take your leftovers from dinner the day before. Otherwise you can make something like muffins or sandwiches with various fillings.

SPECIAL OCCASIONS

If it is close family who will be celebrating, you can find out in advance what will be served and ask whether it is possible to adapt the dish just a little. I tend to skip the appetizer and dessert to make things as easy as possible for the hosts. Once I was attending a 50th birthday party and I knew that tapas would be served. That means a lot of onion and garlic. Instead of bothering the birthday host, I simply brought a box of sushi with me. Perhaps some people thought I was a bit weird, but who cares!

If homemade cakes or pastries are to be served with coffee, you can offer to make a cake. Chocolate Dream Cake (see page 136) with lactose-free cream is a favorite with most people, even those without IBS, so make a huge cake!

For gatherings with good friends and family, you can offer to help with the cooking, or you can bring your own dish or dessert. I always get a lot of praise for the food I make, including from those who do not follow a FODMAP diet, and you'll find the recipes for those desserts in this book.

TRAVELING

I have no problem following a low FODMAP diet when I'm home, but I find it difficult when I am traveling and cannot make my own food. To make it easy, I say that I'm allergic, even though sensitivity to foods with high FODMAP is not an allergy. I explain that I can get very sick if I eat garlic, onion, wheat flour, and dairy—and hope that they will not give me any of these. When I was in China, we fortunately had our own kitchen, but it did not help that much because I didn't understand the ingredient lists on the foods in the store anyway! The next time I go, I will take an allergy card with me. Allergy cards can be ordered on several websites, either with customized text or with standard text from the manufacturer (see Resources, page 172).

It may be smart on planes, trains, and road trips to bring your own ready-made food with you. You can request special food on plane trips, but there are usually no gluten-, dairy-, and onion-free options! Since dry food is the easiest thing to take, you may find yourself eating a lot of gluten-free crackers and low FODMAP carbohydrates, and not enough of the protein and fat that provides a better feeling of fullness. I have solved this by taking leftovers from the freezer with me, and, if possible, cooking meat in advance and then freezing it. The last thing that goes in my bag before I go out the door is a box of frozen food, which will stay cool until I need it. On car and train rides, pack food, along with a frozen bottle of water, in an insulated bag to keep things cool.

If you have the opportunity, stay in an apartment with a kitchen and a refrigerator. That way you can buy food and cook your own meals. This is a bit more difficult in countries where you don't understand the names of the ingredients, but you can pretty much always get hold of plain meat, fish, eggs, and rice!

I would also recommend taking some dry foods you know you can tolerate with you. For example, I always take gluten-free pretzels. These are easy to keep in your bag and to eat on the go. I also often take an egg cooker with me. It is relatively small and you can get eggs pretty much everywhere. Eggs can be eaten with all meals, and are extremely satisfying. Rice noodles are another thing I always have with me. To prepare, soak them in water, drain, add boiling water, let sit for five to ten minutes, and then drain. For more travel tips and my experiences while traveling with the low FODMAP diet, go to my blog: www.nobackpacker.no.

ABOUT THE RECIPES

These are recipes for those who follow a low FODMAP diet, not recipes "without everything." This has been something I have been very aware of, both in my book and my blog, since a low FODMAP diet is already restrictive. I think it is important to have as varied a diet as possible, so my recipes contain eggs, lactose-free milk, butter, and sugar. For those who want to avoid sugar, this can be replaced with other sweeteners, and some lactose-free dairy products can be replaced with, for example, rice milk, oat milk, or almond milk. Please note that soy milk is high FODMAP! Many of the recipes are basic starting points, and you can add your own seasonings or further develop the dishes to suit your taste. Most of the meals in this book are portioned for two adults, unless specified otherwise. There is nothing wrong with serving the whole family low FODMAP food, however, so if you would like to, then simply double the recipe.

I

BREAKFASTS

BREAKFAST MUFFINS

This is a yeast dough that looks like a muffin dough, but bakes like a wheat dough! It is certainly the best gluten-free dough I have ever tasted. These muffins are light, moist, airy, and melt in your mouth.

MAKES 9–10 MUFFINS:

½ cup butter
½ cup lactose-free milk
2 eggs

2 teaspoons dry yeast
1 tablespoon sugar
1 cup gluten-free flour

Preheat the oven to 400°F. Melt the butter in a small saucepan over medium heat, and add the milk. Lightly whisk the eggs and add the hot milk to the bowl. Stir in the yeast, sugar, and finally the flour. The batter should be similar to a pancake batter. Let the dough rise for 45 minutes.

When it has risen, spoon the dough into a greased muffin pan and let the muffins rest for a further 20–30 minutes. Transfer to the oven and bake on the center rack for 10–12 minutes.

TIPS

If you want a coarser version, replace half of the gluten-free flour with oat flour.

Add a bit more sugar for a sweeter dough.

If you want to make it completely dairy-free, substitute the lactose-free milk with water, or oat, rice, or almond milk.

SWEET SCONES

Sweet scones remind me of when we lived in England. On the weekends we often bought scones, clotted cream (thick cream reminiscent of a mixture of cream and butter), and jam and ate them for lunch. Not particularly healthy, but very delicious!

MAKES 6–7 SCONES:

2 cups all-purpose gluten-free flour
⅓ cup sugar
1 teaspoon baking soda
½ cup butter

¾ cup lactose-free yogurt
1 egg
Lactose-free cream and jam, to serve
  (optional)

Preheat the oven to 400°F. Mix the flour, sugar, and baking soda together in a bowl. Crumble the butter into the flour mixture. Beat the yogurt and egg together in a separate bowl and quickly stir into the flour. This dough should not be firm with yeast baking, so it's important that you do not mix it too much!

Line a baking sheet with parchment paper and drop spooonfuls of the batter onto the sheet. Bake for 12–15 minutes.

Serve with lactose-free cream and a little jam, if desired.

TIPS

Mix some finely chopped lactose-free or 70% baking chocolate into the dough.

If you want coarser scones, replace ½ cup of the flour with ½ cup oat flour.

HOMEMADE CREAM CHEESE

This cheese is good on toast or bagels for breakfast, on crackers as a snack, or in sandwiches and salads.

MAKES I PORTION:

4 cups lactose-free milk
3 tablespoons white vinegar
A clean tea towel, cheesecloth, or fine sieve

1 tablespoon chopped chives, or mixed herbs
Salt and pepper, to taste

In a small saucepan, heat the milk almost to boiling point. Remove from the heat, pour in the vinegar, and then return to the burner. The milk will separate quite quickly. If the milk does not separate, pour in a little more vinegar.

When the milk has separated, place the tea towel, cheesecloth, or sieve over a large bowl. Pour the milk through it until you are left with the curd. Gather all the curd in the towel and allow the cheese to drain well. Add the chives and some salt and pepper.

TIP

*If preferred, you can leave the cheese
to drain overnight.*

OVERNIGHT OATS WITH YOGURT AND BERRIES

Overnight oats are really good for those with busy lives: Prepare the oatmeal and cut the fruit and berries in the evening, then breakfast will be ready the next morning! You can also take the oatmeal with you for lunch, stored in a portable container with a lid.

SERVES 1:

½ cup rolled oats
1 tablespoon chia seeds
Lactose-free yogurt
A little vanilla sugar

Fresh berries, such as blueberries,
  raspberries, and strawberries
Chopped pecans or walnuts
Spoonful of maple syrup

Put the oatmeal and chia seeds in a glass jar or bowl and cover with water. Mix together, seal with a lid or cover with plastic wrap, and leave in the refrigerator to soak overnight.

In the morning, mix in lactose-free yogurt and a sprinkling of vanilla sugar to taste. Top with fruit and berries, chopped nuts, and the maple syrup.

———

TIPS

Some people can tolerate more oats than in this recipe, so feel free to customize accordingly.

Substitute fruits such as banana, kiwi, melon, pineapple, and grapes for the berries.

NUT-AND-SEED MUESLI

Muesli is very good with lactose-free yogurt for breakfast, or with a little lactose-free cream as a dessert. I also take it with me when I'm traveling to eat as a snack.

SERVES 2:

¾ cup oatmeal
1 tablespoon sunflower seeds
1 tablespoon pine nuts
1 teaspoon chopped almonds
1 tablespoon pumpkin seeds

1 teaspoon sesame seeds
1 teaspoon maple syrup
1 teaspoon oil
Mixed nuts and seeds that you can tolerate

Preheat the oven to 300°F. Mix all the ingredients in a bowl and then spread over a baking sheet in an even single layer. Bake for approximately 30 minutes. It is important to cook the mixture long enough, for the muesli to get really crisp and develop a nutty flavor.

TIP

The muesli will last for several months if stored in an airtight container.

PANCAKES

Pancakes are often associated with lots of butter and maple syrup—a major calorie bomb! Fortunately, these pancakes can also be eaten with lighter toppings, such as fresh fruit.

MAKES 6–8 PANCAKES:

1 egg
½ cup lactose-free yogurt
½ teaspoon baking soda
⅔ cup all-purpose gluten-free flour

1 teaspoon melted butter, plus extra for cooking
Lactose-free whipped cream and maple syrup, to serve (optional)

Mix the egg and yogurt together in a bowl. Add the baking soda to the flour and stir into egg mixture. Finally, stir in the melted butter. Let the batter rest for 10–15 minutes.

Heat a skillet over medium heat and add butter. Add a ladle of batter and cook until both sides are golden. Repeat until all the batter is used up. Serve with lactose-free cream and maple syrup, if desired.

TIP

Serve as canapés—make small pancakes and top with cheese, ham, a meatball, shrimp, or similar.

VANILLA CRÊPES

I often eat crêpes for breakfast or lunch with a topping. You can try them with bacon or with lactose-free cream and jam or berries. If you divide this recipe by four, you will have just enough for two thicker crêpes.

MAKES 8–10:

4 eggs
2⅛ cups lactose-free milk
2 cups all-purpose gluten-free flour
1 teaspoon vanilla sugar

1 tablespoon sugar
¼ cup melted butter, plus extra
  for cooking
Cinnamon and sugar, to serve

Whisk the eggs together with the milk. Mix the flour, vanilla sugar, and sugar, and pour into the egg mixture a little at a time, while continuously whisking. Stir in the melted butter. Let the batter rest for 10–15 minutes. If the batter becomes too thick, pour in a splash of milk.

Heat a skillet over a medium heat and add butter. Pour in a little batter and cook the crêpe until golden on both sides. Repeat to use all the batter. Serve sprinkled with cinnamon and sugar.

TIPS

For a healthier breakfast version, replace half of the flour with oat flour and/or buckwheat flour (which also doesn't have fructans).

For a savory meal, leave out the sugar in the batter. Make a tomato sauce with ground beef, spoon into a pancake, roll up, sprinkle cheese on top and bake in the oven at 400°F until the cheese has melted.

RASPBERRY SMOOTHIE

Smoothies are healthy choices for breakfast and lunch, and also make a good snack. If you want a slightly thicker variation, add a little oatmeal.

PER PERSON:

3-4 seedless grapes
⅜ cup raspberries
⅓ of a banana
½ cup lactose-free yogurt

Sugar to taste (this depends on whether the yogurt is sweetened or how sweet the fruit is)
Ice cubes

Place all the ingredients, apart from ice cubes, in a blender and process. Pour into a tall glass over ice and serve.

GREEN SMOOTHIE

The avocado and chia seeds make this creamy, but avocado has a FODMAP limit of 1 tablespoon. You can substitute lactose-free milk for the rice milk.

PER PERSON:

1 cup rice milk
1 tablespoon chia seeds
1 tablespoon chopped avocado

4 seedless grapes
A little fresh cilantro

Pour ½ cup of the rice milk into a bowl or glass and add the chia seeds. Soak for at least 30 minutes or, preferably, overnight.

Place the avocado, grapes, and a little fresh cilantro in a blender, along with the rest of the rice milk. Add the soaked chia seeds with the milk and process until smooth. Decorate with a few cilantro leaves on top.

SCRAMBLED EGGS WITH SMOKED SALMON

When I was little, I used to spend summer weekends with my grandparents in the countryside, and we would always have fresh eggs and smoked salmon for breakfast. Now I eat eggs and smoked salmon all year around and it's great both for breakfast and lunch, either alone or with gluten-free bread.

PER PERSON:

2 eggs
2 tablespoons lactose-free cream or milk
1 scallion, green part only
1 teaspoon butter

2–3 thin slices of smoked salmon
Slice gluten-free bread, to serve

Lightly whisk the eggs with the cream or milk until just combined. Finely chop the green tops of the scallion and stir into the eggs.

Heat a skillet over medium–high heat. Melt the butter in the pan, then add the egg mixture. Turn down the heat and let the mixture rest in the pan so that it stiffens slightly. Then take a spatula or wooden spoon and push the egg around the pan until cooked. The eggs will continue to cook after you take them off the heat, so stop cooking a little before you think they are ready.

Serve with the smoked salmon on a toasted slice of gluten-free bread.

TIP

If you want to eat the eggs on their own, add a pinch of salt before serving.

OVEN-BAKED OMELET

This is a great opportunity to use what you have left in your refrigerator, whether it is cooked ham, boiled potatoes, or a mix of vegetables.

SERVES 4:

10 eggs
½ cup lactose-free cream
Chopped chives, or the green
    part of a scallion
⅔-¾ cup sausage, ham, bacon,
    or a mixture

½ teaspoon salt
Pepper
1 cup mild Swiss cheese, grated

Preheat the oven to 400°F. Lightly whisk the eggs and stir in the cream and chives or scallion tops. Cut the meat into cubes and add to the egg mixture. If you are using vegetables, cut these into cubes and add them. If you are using salty ham in the omelet, you do not need to add salt; otherwise season with ½ teaspoon salt and some pepper.

Pour the egg mixture into a small ovenproof dish and bake for 10 minutes. Add the cheese and bake for an additional 10 minutes, or until the cheese has melted.

—

TIP

If you are using sausage, make sure it doesn't contain onion or garlic.

2

SOUPS, SALADS & LIGHT LUNCHES

BEEF SOUP STOCK

Beef stock is extremely useful as a base for soups, stews, and sauces, or as a delicious and warming drink on its own. It is also very nutritious. This version is very concentrated, so it will need diluting when adding to soups.

MAKES 1 QUART:

Approximately 2.2 lbs beef bones and leftover pieces of meat
6¼ cups water
5 carrots

2 scallions or leeks (green parts only)
½ celery stalk (optional)
1–2 tablespoons whole peppercorns
3 teaspoons salt

Put all the ingredients in a large saucepan and bring to a simmer. Allow the stock to simmer for 2–3 hours, or until the liquid has reduced. For a clear broth, skim the foam off the top regularly.

Strain the stock through a large fine-mesh strainer or a colander lined with cheesecloth into a large bowl.

TIP

Lightly salted pork tenderloin works extremely well for making stock, as well as providing lots of delicious meat to use for a soup.

SHRIMP SOUP STOCK

This stock is suitable for both fish soups and sauces. The great thing about it is that it has a short cooking time, so is quick to make.

MAKES ABOUT I QUART:

2¼ lbs shrimp shells
2 tablespoons butter
½ cup white wine (or less)
8⅓ cups water

3 carrots
3 scallions (green parts only)
½ celery stalk

In a large saucepan, sauté the shrimp shells in the butter over medium heat. Add the white wine and boil for approximately 30 seconds. Add the water and the vegetables.

Let the stock simmer for a minimum of 30 minutes but no more than 1½ hours. Strain the stock through a large, fine-mesh strainer, or a colander lined with cheesecloth into a large bowl.

TIP

If you do not have white wine, substitute with
⅛ cup white wine vinegar.

CREAMY CARROT SOUP

I have served this soup for lunch guests, conference participants, and as lunch for a film crew. Everyone was equally surprised and excited by the great taste, even without onions and garlic.

SERVES 2:

4–5 carrots
Approximately 2 cups water
2–4 teaspoons butter
1 teaspoon salt, or 1 bouillon cube
  (make sure it doesn't include onion)

¼–½ teaspoon cayenne pepper
1 tablespoon lactose-free sour cream
Fresh basil or oregano, to serve
Balsamic Glaze (see page 164), to serve

Peel the carrots, cut them into pieces, and simmer for approximately 15 minutes, until tender. Pour off the water, but do not throw it away!

Mash the carrots with a potato masher and add a little butter. Mix the carrot mash with the reserved cooking water until the soup has a nice consistency.

Season with the salt or bouillon and cayenne pepper. Add more water if the consistency is too thick, and bring to a boil.

Just before serving, stir in the sour cream. Add a sprig of fresh basil or oregano, and drizzle over the balsamic glaze to add flavor.

TIPS

Transfer the soup to a thermos and take it on trips.

For a more substantial meal, top the soup with some fried bacon or ham.

CLASSIC TOMATO SOUP

Most people are quite familiar with supermarket tomato soup. I don't mind using ready-made products occasionally, and as we all have busy and hectic lives, the convenience is worth it! Unfortunately, however, most commercial soups contain wheat flour and/or onion and garlic. Onion- and gluten-free tomato soups are available, but I've found that it is just as easy, and so much better, to make your own tomato soup from scratch.

SERVES 2:

1 scallion (green parts only)
A neutral oil, such as canola or corn oil
2½ cups canned chopped tomatoes
½ cup water
1 tablespoon Balsamic Glaze (see page 164)
½ teaspoon sugar (because the tomatoes have a lot of acidity, you need sweetness)

1 bouillon cube (without onion/garlic) or ½ teaspoon salt
Salt, pepper, and cayenne pepper
Fresh or dried oregano and/or basil
¼ cup lactose-free cream
Croutons (see page 97), to serve (optional)

Sauté the scallion in a drizzle of the oil in a deep saucepan, and add the tomatoes and water. Bring to a boil, then simmer for 10 minutes.

Purée the soup with a hand-held blender and add in the balsamic glaze and sugar. Season with salt or bouillon, pepper, cayenne pepper, and the herbs.

Stir in the cream and bring the soup to a boil again. If the soup is very thick, add a little more water. Serve with croutons, if desired.

TIPS

If you want a slightly lighter version, replace the cream with lactose-free milk.

Add meatballs to the soup. Make ground pork patties (see page 120) or use ground chicken. Shape the meatballs in your hands and gently add them to the soup. Allow the soup to simmer for 10 minutes. Make sure the meatballs are well cooked before serving.

FISH SOUP WITH
SALMON BALLS

This soup can be made more extravagant with the addition of
different types of fish and seafood, such as shrimp, mussels, and scallops.

SERVES 3–4:

Salmon balls:
Salmon Fishcake mixture (see page 66)

Soup:
4 potatoes
4 carrots
2 scallions (green parts only)

4¼ cups water with 2 bouillon cubes
    or 2 teaspoons salt, or Shrimp Soup
    Stock (see page 49)
2 tablespoons rice flour
½ cup lactose-free sour cream
¼ cup lactose-free cream
Croutons (see page 97), to serve

Peel the carrots and potatoes and wash the scallions. Cut the vegetables into
chunks. Add to boiling stock in a saucepan and allow the vegetables to simmer for
5 minutes. Remove from the heat.

In a separate bowl, mix the rice flour with a little cold water until it forms a lump-
free ball and then add this to the soup, mixing it well, while bringing the water to a
boil again. Simmer for 5 minutes.

Make small fish balls from the fishcake mixture, add it to the soup and cook for
5–6 minutes. Make sure they are thoroughly cooked before serving.

Mix the sour cream and cream into the soup, then warm it up again but do not
allow it to boil, as the cream will separate. Season with salt and pepper. Serve with
the croutons.

TIP

*For a lighter version, you can use lactose-free milk
instead of the sour cream and cream.*

RAINBOW QUINOA SALAD

Although quinoa is low FODMAP, some people do react to it, so do not eat this salad for the first 6–8 weeks of a low FODMAP diet. You can eat it during the reintroduction phase, when you can check for any reaction.

SERVES 3–4:

¾ cup uncooked quinoa
3 tomatoes
½ red bell pepper
½ yellow bell pepper
Small handful fresh cilantro

3 tablespoons raspberry extract
3 tablespoons extra virgin olive oil
¼–⅓ cup grated Parmesan
Freshly ground pepper

Cook the quinoa as directed on the package and allow to cool. Dice the tomatoes and peppers. Roughly chop the cilantro leaves and mix the tomatoes, peppers, and cilantro with the quinoa. Pour in the raspberry extract and olive oil and let the mixture sit for 30 minutes, so the quinoa can absorb all the flavors.

Mix in the grated Parmesan and ground pepper just before serving.

TIPS

*Serve as a cold lunch or as a side dish
with fish or meat.*

*Add cooked, chopped chicken or another meat to
make a more substantial dish.*

RAW SPROUTED SALAD

This salad is delicious as a lunchtime meal or as a side dish to accompany meat or fish for dinner.

SERVES 2–3:

3 carrots
Large handful green cabbage leaves
3 cups alfalfa sprouts
½ cup bean sprouts

Dressing:
1 teaspoon lemon juice
1 teaspoon sweet mustard
3 tablespoons olive oil
Freshly ground pepper

Peel, wash and grate the carrots. Finely chop the green cabbage and mix with the carrots, alfalfa sprouts, and bean sprouts.

For the dressing, whisk together the lemon juice and mustard, and drizzle in the oil while continuing to whisk. Pour the dressing over the salad, grind over a little pepper, and serve.

CREAMY PASTA SALAD
WITH CHICKEN

You can use any vegetables you like, and can tolerate, in this salad. Please note that two sun-dried tomatoes are low FODMAP, so you will still stay in the elimination plan if you share this portion with one other person. You can prepare the pasta and dressing the day before, but wait to mix everything together until just before it is served.

SERVES 2-3:

4 cups cold, cooked gluten-free pasta
3 tomatoes
¼ cucumber
½ red bell pepper
¼ head iceberg lettuce
Skinless, boneless chicken breasts, grilled
Alfalfa sprouts and 1 tablespoon chopped avocado, to garnish

Dressing:
3 sun-dried tomatoes (make sure there is no garlic)
⅜ cup lactose-free cream
4 tablespoons mayonnaise
A few chives, chopped
1 teaspoon white wine vinegar
½ teaspoon cayenne pepper
½ teaspoon paprika

First make the dressing. Finely chop the sun-dried tomatoes and place in a blender with the remaining ingredients. Process to combine well. Stir through the cold pasta until evenly coated.

Chop the tomatoes, cucumber, bell pepper, lettuce, and chicken. Just before serving, mix with the pasta. Top the salad with the alfalfa sprouts and chopped avocado, and serve.

TIPS

Customize the recipe by adding ham, bacon, or a mixture of different meats.

If you have any left over, this salad is great for lunch the following day.

ARUGULA AND SERRANO HAM SALAD

I love this salad. It's great as a simple lunch or as a light evening meal. Serrano ham is low FODMAP, but be aware that some people do react to it.

SERVES 1:

2–3 thin slices Serrano ham
1 tomato, sliced
Handful of arugula

1 tablespoon Balsamic Glaze (see page 164)
1 tablespoon good olive oil
¼ cup grated Parmesan cheese

Place the Serrano ham on a plate, then arrange the tomato slices and arugula over the ham. Drizzle over the balsamic glaze and olive oil, sprinkle on the Parmesan cheese, and serve.

HALLOUMI AND RASPBERRY SALAD

Halloumi is a salty and solid white cheese made from sheep milk. It is naturally low in lactose and can therefore be eaten on a low FODMAP diet. The cheese will not melt when you heat it, and is great cooked on a grill, under a broiler, or fried in a skillet.

SERVES 2:

Handful of salad greens per person
3 tomatoes
About 8 oz halloumi
3 tablespoons good olive oil

1 tablespoon balsamic vinegar
1 cup fresh raspberries
Fresh oregano, to serve

Place the salad leaves on a serving plate. Cut the tomatoes into cubes and scatter over the leaves.

Cut the halloumi into slices and fry it quickly in a skillet or on a griddle. Place it on top of the salad. Mix the oil and vinegar together and pour over the dressing.

Roughly chop the raspberries, sprinkle over the salad with a little oregano, and serve.

BEEF, SPINACH, AND CARROT RICE BOWL

The first time I was in Japan, I discovered this simple meal. I have used spinach and carrot here, but you may want to use other vegetables. The meat can also be varied, according to your taste.

SERVES 3–4:

1 lb tender beef
1 tablespoon butter
2 carrots, grated
3 cups chopped fresh spinach
3 tablespoons soy sauce
1½ teaspoons sugar
1 teaspoon grated fresh ginger

1 tablespoon water
½–1 teaspoon chili powder (depending on how much you like and can tolerate)
6 cups cooked brown rice
1 cup canned bean sprouts
Sesame seeds, to garnish

Cut the beef into strips. In a skillet over high heat, add the butter, then stir-fry the beef and half the grated carrot. Add the spinach. Mix the soy sauce with the sugar, ginger, and water, and add to the stir-fry. Let it rest for 1-2 minutes. Add chili to taste.

Divide the brown rice between small bowls. Place the meat, the remaining raw grated carrot, and a few bean sprouts on top of the rice. Sprinkle over some sesame seeds, and serve.

SALMON SASHIMI

This is a really easy and delicious meal with all the flavors of sushi, which is fortunately low FODMAP.

SERVES 2:

1¼ cups uncooked rice
10 oz very fresh raw salmon

Sauce:
⅔ cup soy sauce
1 tablespoon lemon juice
1 tablespoon orange juice

Boil the rice as directed on the package. Divide between plates. Cut the salmon into thin slices and arrange over the rice.

Mix the sauce ingredients together and serve on the side.

TIPS

If you are not fond of raw salmon, divide it into serving sizes and either cook it over medium heat until cooked through, or sear it on each side so that it is cooked on the outside and raw on the inside.

Add fresh herbs like cilantro and chives to the sauce, or use to garnish the fish and rice before serving.

If you don't have lemon juice or orange juice, substitute pure soy sauce.

SALMON FISHCAKES

My son loves these fishcakes so much he's told all his friends about them. They are great to keep in the freezer for quick meals, when children or friends come over to visit.

MAKES 10–12:

14 oz salmon filet
1 egg
¼ cup lactose-free heavy cream
½ teaspoon dried ginger (optional)
1½ tablespoons balsamic vinegar or
  lemon juice
½–1 teaspoons salt

½ teaspoon pepper, chili powder, and/or
  cayenne pepper, to season
3-4 scallions (green part only)
2 tablespoons butter or oil for frying
10-12 boiled potatoes, lactose-free
  sour cream, dill, and lemon wedges,
  to serve

Put the salmon, egg, cream, ginger, if using, balsamic vinegar or lemon, and salt and pepper or chili powder into a blender and process until finely chopped. Add the scallion and mix well.

Cook a small portion of the mixture and taste to see if you need to add a little more salt and/or pepper. Heat butter or oil in a skillet over medium heat and drop in tablespoonfuls of the mixture. Fry on each side for 2–3 minutes. Do not overcook, as they will become dry. Serve 2 fishcakes with 2–3 potatoes per person, sour cream, dill, and lemon.

TIPS

*For an extra kick, add a little grated
horseradish to the fishcake mixture.*

*Create a delicious fish burger! Use Focaccia
(see page 92), and add a slice of tomato, some
lettuce, a little lactose-free sour cream, and a
salmon patty.*

HAM AND SPINACH QUICHE

This is the perfect dish for entertaining. Quiches can be made the day before and you can customize them, making several kinds with different types of meat and/or vegetables.

SERVES 4:

Pie crust:
½ cup butter
1⅓ cups all-purpose gluten-free flour
4 tablespoons water
Ceramic pie weights

Filling:
4 eggs
1¼ cups lactose-free cream
1 cup grated cheese
10½ oz ham
3 scallions, green parts only
¾ cup chopped fresh spinach
1⅛ cups chopped broccoli florets, if you
    can tolerate it
Thyme, to garnish

Preheat the oven to 400°F. Make the pie crust. Crumble the butter into the flour and add the water. Knead the dough until firm. Let the dough rest for 30 minutes. Roll or hand press the dough into a 9-inch pie pan. (Gluten-free dough is hard to roll, so I prefer to hand press the dough.) Prick the bottom with a fork and cover the crust with parchment paper. Put the pie weights into the pan. This will prevent the pastry from shrinking or forming bubbles while it bakes! Pre-cook the crust for 10 minutes. Remove the pie weights and parchment paper.

Now make the filling. Mix the eggs, cream, and cheese together. Chop the ham and scallion into small pieces and add them to the egg mixture, together with the spinach and broccoli, if using. Pour the filling into the pie pan and bake the quiche on the center rack for approximately 30–40 minutes, until the filling is firm.

TIPS

Substitute chicken for the ham in the recipe.

If you can tolerate it, serve the quiche with fresh greens or a vegetable salad dressed with Sour Cream Dressing (see page 163).

CHOUX PASTRY SANDWICH ROLLS

The great thing about making rolls from choux pastry is that there is no sugar in the dough, and the rolls make great substitutes for bread.

MAKES 6:

¼ cup butter
1 cup water
½ cup all-purpose gluten-free flour

2 eggs
Sliced ham, tomato, chopped chives,
Potato Salad (see page 84), to serve

Preheat the oven to 400°F. Place the butter and water in a saucepan and bring to a boil. Sift the flour into the pan and stir continuously while the saucepan remains on the heat. Make sure that the butter does not separate from the flour.

Remove the pan from the heat and let the mixture rest for approximately 5 minutes. Add in the eggs, one at a time, thoroughly mixing after each one. It will seem as if the mixture couldn't possibly become a dough, but just keep mixing. You'll suddenly notice that the dough will come together and you'll have a nice mixture that will not separate.

Cover a baking sheet with parchment paper. Using a pastry bag, pipe—or spoon— six rolls onto the sheet. Keep in mind that they will almost double in size as they bake! Bake in the oven on the center rack for 25–30 minutes. DO NOT give in to the temptation to open the oven door before the rolls are baked, or they will collapse. Make sure they bake fully before removing them from the oven, or they may also collapse. Once baked, rest on a wire rack until cool.

When cool, slice the rolls in half. Fill with the ham, potato salad, and tomato, sprinkle with chives, and serve.

TIP

For a sweet option, fill the pastry with Vanilla Bean Cream (see page 126) and drizzle with a sugar glaze (confectioners' sugar mixed with a few drops of water).

EGG SALAD SANDWICH

Egg salad is delicious when served alongside a plain green salad, but it also makes a very good sandwich filling. The best part is that it is very easy to make!

SERVES 2:

3½ tablespoons mayonnaise
3 tablespoons lactose-free sour cream
2 hard-boiled eggs
3–3½ oz ham, chopped
1 scallion, green parts only
Salt and pepper, to taste

Vinegar or lemon juice (optional)
Focaccia (see page 92), or other gluten-free
   bread
1 tomato, sliced
Fresh thyme, to garnish

Make the mayonnaise (see page 162) or use store-bought mayonnaise. Mix the mayonnaise with the sour cream.

Roughly chop the hard-boiled eggs and mix with the ham and scallion, reserving a pinch for garnish. Add the mayonnaise mixture and combine until the eggs and ham are nicely coated.

Season with salt and pepper. To add even more flavor, add a few drops of vinegar or lemon juice to the egg mixture. Use to fill the focaccia, layering with slices of tomato, and sprinking over the reserved scallion and thyme.

TIPS

Substitute shrimp or bacon for the ham.

*If you eat this with a plain green salad, you do not
need any extra salad dressing.*

WHOLE-GRAIN WAFFLE SANDWICH

These waffles are a great alternative to bread, if you do not have any in the house and need a quick breakfast, lunch, or dinner. They can be eaten as they are or used as sandwich bread with ham, cheese, or any other low FODMAP filling you like.

MAKES 3–4 WAFFLES:

2 eggs
⅔ cup lactose-free milk
⅓ cup all-purpose gluten-free flour
⅓ cup buckwheat flour
2½ tablespoons oat flour

1 teaspoon baking powder
⅓ cup oil
8 oz sliced ham
1 portion Homemade Cream Cheese
(see page 34)

In a bowl, whisk the eggs and milk together, then mix in the rest of the ingredients, except the ham and cream cheese, until you have a lump-free batter. Let rest for 10–15 minutes.

Cook the waffles in a waffle iron until golden, approximately 2–3 minutes each.

When ready to serve, cut each waffle in half and serve filled with slices of ham and cream cheese. The waffles can be enjoyed hot or cold.

Note: You can use pre-made oat flour, or you can make your own by pulsing oats in a blender until they become flour.

TIPS

You may want to make the waffle batter the day before. If the batter thickens, add some extra milk.

These waffles are best if you eat them straight off the waffle iron!

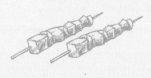

3

SNACKS & SIDES

CHICKEN KEBABS WITH SERRANO HAM

There is not a lot of flavor in ground chicken meat, but combined with Serrano ham, these chicken kebabs are delicious!

SERVES 3–4:

3 oz Serrano ham
14 oz ground chicken meat
1 egg
¼ cup lactose-free heavy cream

½ teaspoon chili powder
½ teaspoon salt
½ teaspoon pepper
Wooden kebab skewers

Preheat the oven to 400°F. Cut the Serrano ham into small pieces and mix well with the ground chicken meat. Mix in the egg, cream, and spices until you have a smooth mixture.

Cook a small sample in a skillet to taste for seasoning.

Squeeze a small handful of the chicken mixture around each skewer and flash-fry in a hot skillet until golden brown on both sides.

Place the kebabs on a baking sheet and cook them in the oven for 10–15 minutes. Make sure the meat is cooked thoroughly!

TIPS

Serve with fried potatoes or rice noodles.

Shape the meat like sausages, without skewers, and serve with Pancakes (see page 38) or Rice Tortillas (see page 80).

Bacon can be substituted for Serrano ham.

RICE TORTILLAS

If you miss making tacos with wheat tortillas, then these homemade rice tortillas are incredibly quick and easy to make and are a great substitute. The best thing about them is that the only flour you need is rice flour!

MAKES 4-5 SMALL TORTILLAS:

½ cup water
1 teaspoon oil
¼ teaspoon salt
½ cup rice flour

To serve:
15 oz ground beef
Taco seasoning, without onion and
  garlic
3 oz mild Cheddar cheese, grated
4–5 tablespoons salsa
8 tablespoons sour cream
Iceberg lettuce, shredded
Cilantro, to garnish

Place the water, oil, and salt in a small saucepan, and bring to a boil. Just before it reaches a rolling boil, add the flour while continuously stirring.

Once combined, remove the dough from the saucepan, and divide it into 4–5 even pieces. Place a piece of dough between two baking sheets, and press firmly to thin out the dough. Gently loosen the dough from the baking sheets and cook them over medium–high heat in a dry skillet. The tortillas will bubble a little when they are cooked, but this is quite normal and they will flatten as soon as you remove them from the skillet. Place the tortillas inside a clean dishcloth once cooked to keep them warm.

Meanwhile, fry ground beef in a hot skillet with taco seasoning for 2–3 minutes, then pile on top of the tortillas with salsa, sour cream, shredded lettuce, grated cheese and cilantro.

TIP

*Do not give into the temptation to make the tortillas
too thin and too big. If they get too thin, they
become dry, and if they are too big you will have
trouble getting the dough off the baking sheets before
cooking them!*

SPRING ROLLS

The spring rolls you buy most always contain onions and garlic. So, it's great to know that you can make your own low FODMAP spring rolls!

MAKES 25-30:

30 dried rice paper sheets
(sold online)
Oil for frying

The marinade:
½ cup ketchup
3 tablespoons Balsamic Glaze (see page 164)
⅓ cup olive oil
1 teaspoon salt
3 teaspoons soy sauce
1 teaspoon pepper

1 teaspoon ginger
1 teaspoon sesame oil
1 teaspoon cayenne pepper
1–2 teaspoons chili powder

Filling:
1 package rice noodles (375 g or 12¾ oz dried)
5-6 large carrots
1 head iceberg lettuce/another lettuce
1-1⅓ cup ground meat, your preference
2-3 scallions, only the green part (as much as you want and tolerate)

For the marinade, whisk all the ingredients together to combine. Taste to see if you need more spices. Remember it will be milder once dispersed through the rest of the ingredients. Place the noodles in a shallow bowl and cover with boiling water. Leave for 4–5 minutes. Drain and rinse with cold water, pulling the noodles apart so that they don't stick together. Thinly slice the carrots and cut the lettuce into thin strips. Cook the ground meat, and mix in the noodles, marinade, lettuce, carrots, and scallions.

Rinse the rice paper sheets one by one by dipping them in a large bowl of water. Place the rehydrated sheets on a wet platter, making sure not to overlap them, so that they don't stick together. Once the rice sheets have become soft and yellowish, after approximately 1 minute, place about 1¹/₂ tablespoons of filling in the middle of each. Take each filled rice paper and roll it over once. Fold each of the sides in and then roll again.

Heat a frying pan with corn oil or another neutral tasting oil that can withstand high heat. Fry the spring rolls in batches for 2–3 minutes on each side, being careful not to overcrowd the pan.

SUMMER ROLLS

I have to admit that I was not particularly excited the first time I ate Vietnamese summer rolls. Last time I was in France, I decided to try them again and bought one for lunch—it was very good! I decided that I would try to make something similar when I got home.

MAKES 10-12:

8.8 oz thin rice noodles
12 large rice paper sheets
20–24 marinated, cooked shrimp (see
    page 114) cooked ham, chicken or
    other cooked meat

10-12 large lettuce leaves
2 grated carrots
Mint leaves
Soy sauce

Place the rice noodles in a shallow bowl and cover with boiling water. Keep the noodles in the water for 4–5 minutes and then rinse under cold water so they don't get too sticky. Rinse the sheets of rice paper under cold running water and place them on a clean, wet dishcloth, so that the paper becomes soft. Take care not to overlap the sheets so they don't stick together.

Place a lettuce leaf and some mint leaves on each sheet of paper. Put some rice noodles, carrot, and meat/shrimp on the mint leaves and roll the rice paper as tightly as you can. Serve with soy sauce as a dip.

TIPS

Here you can use what you like and tolerate, and it's only your imagination that will limit what you can pack into your rice paper! How about pork, ham, or perhaps pan-fried duck breast? You could even use leftovers from another dinner.

Because I like using marinated shrimp, my summer rolls become a little greasier and not as white as the ones from a restaurant, but the flavor is heavenly!

POTATO SALAD

This potato salad is so much more flavorful than store-bought versions, and it is best if left for a few hours in the refrigerator before serving.

SERVES 3–4:

7 medium potatoes
¾ lactose-free sour cream
Fresh chives

Place the whole potatoes in a large saucepan and cover with water. Boil until cooked through, then drain and peel while hot (this is not essential, but it is easier to peel freshly cooked potatoes). Let the potatoes cool completely, and then cut them into cubes.

Pour the sour cream into a bowl, then add the chopped chives and mix until combined. Add the cubed potatoes little by little, stirring gently to ensure the sour cream and chives evenly coat the potatoes. Refrigerate until ready to eat.

TIPS

For a smoother taste, you can add a tablespoon of Mayonnaise (see page 162) and a pinch of sugar.

The salad can be made up to a day in advance.

POTATOES TWO WAYS

It is said that potatoes can be used for everything and that is indeed true.
The potato is a very versatile root vegetable and can be varied indefinitely.
That's why it's very good that the potato is low FODMAP!

AS A SNACK OR SIDE DISH:

Roasted potatoes:
2-3 raw potatoes per person
½ tablespoon oil per potato
Salt and pepper
Herbes de Provence

Fried potatoes in the frying pan:
2-3 potatoes per person
½ tablespoon oil per potato

Roasted potatoes: Preheat the oven to 390°F. Wash, scrub, and dry the potatoes
and cut them in halves or quarters, depending on how large they are. Grease
a roasted pan with some oil and toss the potato pieces with the rest of the oil.
Sprinkle with salt, pepper, and Herbes de Provence and bake for 30-40 minutes
until the potatoes are tender. This can vary from oven to oven and how large your
potatoes are.

Fried potatoes in the frying pan: Wash and peel the potatoes, then pat dry with
a clean dishcloth or paper towel. Cut them into strips or small squares. Put the
frying pan on medium heat and heat the oil. Fry the potatoes for 10-15 minutes or
until they are tender. If you think the potatoes are too oily, place them on a paper
towel to drain.

TIPS

*You can also add finely chopped fresh herbs such as
rosemary, basil, and oregano to the potatoes.*

*Peel some carrots, cut them into small cubes, and fry
with the potatoes.*

Add leftover meat and vegetables to the potatoes.

CARROT PURÉE

Carrot purée is a delicious accompaniment for most meat dishes and is a good substitute for sauce. I often serve carrot purée when we have guests, and it never fails. They are highly intrigued by the "orange" that tastes so good!

SERVES 3-4:

10 big carrots
2–2½ tablespoons butter
Pinch of salt or bouillon powder
   (without onions)

2 tablespoons sour cream
Thyme, or other fresh herbs, to garnish

Peel the carrots and roughly chop them into pieces. Place the carrots in a medium saucepan and cover with boiling water. Cook over medium–high heat until tender, about 15 minutes.

Drain off the water and mash the carrots with a immersion blender. Add the butter, salt, or bouillon powder, and the sour cream, and then stir to combine thoroughly. Garnish with thyme or other fresh herbs before serving.

———

TIP

Add in chicken or another meat.

SAUTÉED GREEN BEANS WITH CARROTS AND BACON

This salad is delicious as a side for meat or fish. Green beans are low FODMAP, up to ½ cup. If you are very sensitive to polyols, you may react to a small amount. If this is the case, use carrots or fewer beans.

SERVES 2-3:

3½ oz bacon
1 scallion, only the green parts

4 carrots
3½ oz green beans

Cut the bacon into pieces and fry in a skillet with a little butter. Chop the green part of the scallion and cut the carrots into sticks. Put the carrots, green beans, and scallion into the skillet, and sauté them with the bacon for approximately 5 minutes.

Serve as an accompaniment to any type of meat.

TIP

If you make this dish without bacon, salt the vegetables a bit.

FOCACCIA

I have become very fond of using gluten-free pizza dough in this recipe for focaccia. When it was time to take photos of the portion-size focaccia, the photographer wondered if it really was focaccia, as she thought focaccia was supposed to look like long flatbread. I have made the dough like a long flatbread, but I think this recipe is best as a small portion bread.

MAKES 1 MEDIUM FLATBREAD OR 4 INDIVIDUAL FLATBREADS:

1¼ lactose-free milk
1¼ cups lactose-free sour cream or
   lactose-free Quark
1 teaspoon sugar
2 tablespoons olive oil
2 teaspoons dry yeast
2½-3 cups gluten-free light flour

3 teaspoons psyllium husk (sold online)
½ teaspoon baker's ammonia (ammonium
   carbonate)
Rosemary, olive oil, and sea salt, to garnish
Balsamic Glaze (see page 164) and olive oil,
   and Mayonnaise (see page 162), to serve

Place the milk and sour cream, or Quark, in a large saucepan and heat gently. Add the sugar, oil, and yeast to the liquid, and whisk until the yeast is dissolved. Sift the gluten-free flour, psyllium husk, and baker's ammonia into a large bowl or food processor, then add the liquids. Mix by hand or process until combined. Let the dough rise for an hour in a warm, dry place.

If making a large focaccia, transfer the dough to a loaf pan, then press your fingertips into the surface of the dough to make shallow indentations. Let the dough rise for an additional hour.

If you choose to make individual focaccia, divide the dough into quarters, press it gently into small loaves, and place them on an oiled baking sheet. Press your fingertips into the surface of the focaccia to make shallow indentations. Let the dough rise for an additional hour.

Once the dough has risen, preheat the oven to 425°F, if making a large loaf, or 400°F, if making individual flatbreads. Sprinkle a little olive oil, salt, and roughly chopped rosemary over the top of the bread before baking.

Bake the large focaccia for 30–40 minutes, or unti golden brown on top. The individual portions of bread must be baked for 20–25 minutes. Serve drizzled with two tablespoons of balsamic glaze, olive oil, and mayonnaise on the side.

SAVORY MUFFINS WITH CARROT, HAM & CHEESE

This was one of the first recipes I made when I began the low FODMAP diet. I've made these muffins many times since, and this version is one of the best!

MAKES 10–12:

4 eggs
½ cup olive or sunflower oil
½ cup lactose-free plain yogurt
⅔ cup oat flour*
⅓ cup all-purpose gluten-free flour
2 teaspoons sugar
1 teaspoon baking soda

½ cup grated carrot
1 teaspoon dried oregano or Herbes de Provence
½ cup ham, cut into small cubes, or bacon, chopped
Swiss cheese to sprinkle on top

Preheat the oven to 325°F. Whisk the eggs. Mix the oil and yogurt with the eggs, and add the flours, sugar, baking soda, grated carrot, dried herbs, and ham or bacon. Line a muffin pan with paper liners, then pour in the batter, making sure not to overfill, and sprinkle grated cheese on top.

Bake on the center rack of the oven for 16–18 minutes.

Note: You can use pre-made oat flour, or you can make your own by processing the oats in a blender until fine.

TIPS

These are perfect to take on a trip!

You can make your own muffin cups to store and transport the muffins. Press a piece of parchment paper around a glass, or anything else that fits, to form the mold. Pour the muffin batter into the lined mold and bake.

OAT ENERGY BARS

This recipe was created before I went on a trip to Morocco. The fear of getting sick drove me to come up with an energy bar that I could carry in my purse.

MAKES 8 MEDIUM BARS:

⅛ cup oats
⅛ cup Cheerios™ cereal
¼ tablespoons sunflower seeds
¼ tablespoons pumpkin seeds
¼ tablespoons pine nuts

2 tablespoons sugar
3½ tablespoons oil
1 egg
4 tablespoons lactose-free cooking chocolate

Preheat oven to 325°F. Place all the ingredients in a large bowl, and mix until combined. Spoon the batter onto a baking sheet lined with parchment paper. Lightly shape the mixture into bar shapes, and bake on the center rack of the oven for 25–30 minutes.

The bars are best when they are well cooked, almost burned, as they will get crispy, which will bring out a nutty flavor in the seeds! They will remain fresh in an airtight container for up to 2 weeks.

Note: Pumpkin seeds, sunflower seeds, and pine nuts are all low FODMAP, up to ½–¾ cup. As one serving of these bars is not more than ½ cup, however, you should be able to eat these without feeling sick!

Cheerios are not 100 percent gluten-free. If you have celiac disease, you can replace Cheerios with gluten-free oats.

TIPS

Pack the bars in a sealed container lined with parchment paper (so they do not break) if you want to take them with you on a trip.

For a quick breakfast on the go: crush a bar and mix it with dairy-free yogurt.

CROUTONS

As most people on a gluten-free diet will know, wheat-free bread often dries out before you're able to finish the whole loaf. Here's a way to use "old" gluten-free bread!

Gluten-free bread
Oil

Cut the bread into cubes and fry the pieces in oil in a frying pan over high heat. Once golden brown and crisp, place the croutons on a paper towel to absorb the excess oil.

CRISPBREAD

Traveling with gluten-free bread can be difficult, as it quickly goes stale. But if you make crispbread instead, you will have enough bread for a whole vacation!

Gluten-free bread, sliced as thinly as you can

Preheat the oven to 175-200°F. Place the bread on a baking sheet, ensuring that the slices don't overlap. Depending on the size of your oven, you may want to bake a few trays at a time.

Place the baking sheet in the oven and bake the bread for 2–3 hours, depending on how thick the slices are. Open the oven, from time to time, so that any moisture is released.

Once the bread is completely dried out, remove the trays and let them cool. Store the crispbread in an airtight container and they will last for several weeks.

SALTY CRACKERS

Delicious plain, or with some butter or cheese on top!

MAKES 25–30 CRACKERS:

1¾ cups gluten-free light flour
½ teaspoon baking powder
½ cup grated Parmesan cheese
½ cup butter

2 eggs
Water
1 egg for brushing on the crackers
Sea salt flakes

Preheat the oven to 400°F. Sift the flour and baking powder into a large bowl, add the Parmesan cheese, and stir to combine. Rub the butter into the dry ingredients with your fingertips until it forms a dough. Lightly whisk the two eggs and add to the mixing bowl, then bring the dough together, gently kneading until combined. If you think the dough is too dry, add a little water until it is smooth.

Line a baking sheet with parchment paper. Take approximately an ⅛th of a cup of the dough, and roll it into a round thin cracker directly onto the parchment paper. After rolling out all of the dough, brush the tray of crackers with the lightly whisked egg, prick each one with a fork and then sprinkle over a generous pinch of sea salt. Be sure to only brush the crackers with the egg just before they go in the oven, otherwise they will not get crisp enough.

Place the baking sheet in the oven on the center rack, and bake the crackers for 4–6 minutes until crisp and golden brown.

The crackers will last approximately one week in a sealed container.

—

TIP

If you are nauseous and unable to eat anything, but need sustenance, these crackers can be lifesavers!

4

MAIN MEALS

HOMEMADE PASTA

When I began making homemade gluten-free pasta, I was not sure if I'd be able to do it. I was worried that gluten-free pasta dough might not be elastic enough or it would clump together. To my surprise, it was actually quite easy to make.

SERVES 2:

¾ cup gluten-free flour, plus extra for kneading and coating

1 large egg
1 tablespoon oil

Put the flour into a large bowl. Make a small well in the center and pour the egg and oil into the middle. Fold the flour into the liquid, mixing in a little at a time, while stirring in the middle. Don't give up, even if the flour does not become fine and smooth; if you have lumps they can be kneaded out. Transfer the dough to a lightly-floured surface and knead it, for a few minutes, into a smooth but quite compact dough. Transfer the dough to a plastic bag and leave it for 20 minutes.

Set up the pasta machine. Take a section of the dough, press it flat, put it into the machine, and crank away. Begin on the most "open" setting and then move to the next setting and run the dough through. Continue until the dough is as thin as you like. I stop at setting no. 6.

Then run the dough through the cutting part of the machine to make tagliatelle. Use plenty of gluten-free flour to coat the dough as it goes through the machine.

The cooking time for fresh pasta is approximately 2–4 minutes, depending on how thick the pasta is, and your preference for consistency.

TIPS

If you do not have a pasta machine, roll out the dough with a rolling pin and cut it with a knife.

Leftover uncooked pasta can be dried for one hour on the countertop and stored in a sealed container in the refrigerator. It will keep for 2–3 days.

LASAGNA PIE

My family loves this lasagna. It can be easily frozen, as a whole pie, or in individual servings, for quick weekday meals.

SERVES 5-6:

Béchamel sauce:
See page 153

Meat sauce:
2 tablespoons oil, plus 1 teaspoon for greasing the baking dish
½ cup grated carrot
1 lb ground beef
3½ oz tomato purée
2½ cups canned chopped tomatoes
⅓–⅔ cups water

1½ teaspoons sugar
1 teaspoon grated fresh ginger
2 teaspoons Italian herbs (oregano, thyme, basil)
1 teaspoon cayenne pepper
1–1½ teaspoons salt
8 oz rice sheets or other gluten-free lasagna sheets
5½–7 oz mild Cheddar cheese, grated

Preheat the oven to 400°F. Heat the oil in a skillet over medium heat and cook the carrot and ground beef. Add the tomato purée, canned tomatoes, and ⅓–⅔ cups water. Add the sugar, ginger, herbs, and spices, and adjust to taste. I prefer the sauce to be a little salty and spicy to keep the dish balanced.

Grease a round, 10-inch ovenproof baking dish, add layers of the béchamel sauce, meat sauce, and pasta sheets, layer by layer. Top with the cheese. Transfer the dish to the oven and bake the pie on the bottom rack for approximately 30 minutes.

TIPS

Gouda and other hard cheeses are low in lactose, so you do not need to use special lactose-free cheese.

You may like to serve the lasagna with a side salad and/or some bread, such as Focaccia (see page 92).

WHITE PIZZA WITH CHICKEN

Many people are used to pizza with tomato sauce, but this version is made without the sauce, which makes the dough a little crispier. Of course, you can use tomato sauce, but then you'll need to put the cheese on top, rather than under it.

MAKES 3–5 INDIVIDUAL PIZZAS:

Pizza dough:
See Focaccia recipe, page 92
Gluten-free flour, for dusting

Topping:
3–4 tablespoons ketchup
1 teaspoon Balsamic Glaze (see page 164)

1–2 teaspoons salt
1–2 teaspoons pepper
Cayenne pepper (to taste)
Approx. 2 cups grated mild Cheddar or mozzarella cheese
1–2 chicken fillets
8 oz bacon, chopped
Fresh thyme or scallions (green parts only), to garnish

Make the dough as for the focaccia on page 92.

Preheat the oven to 430°F. Sprinkle approximately ½ cup of flour onto your work surface and knead the dough until it is smooth. Since gluten-free dough is very sticky and difficult to roll out, it is easiest to put some oil on your hands and then press out the dough into individual pizzas, straight onto a greased baking sheet or parchment paper. Let the dough rise for approximately 30 minutes. The number of pizzas you will get from the dough depends on how thick you choose to make them. You can also make one large pizza.

Half-bake the pizza bases for 4–5 minutes on the center rack of the oven.

Make the topping. Mix the ketchup, balsamic glaze, and spices to make a marinade. Cut the chicken into small pieces and add them to the marinade; let the mixture rest for a few minutes. Sprinkle the grated cheese over the part-baked pizzas, then add the marinated chicken and top with the bacon pieces.

Bake the pizzas for 14–18 minutes, until the cheese has melted and the chicken is thoroughly cooked. Scatter with the thyme or scallions before serving.

CHILI BEEF NOODLES

Rice noodles can be bought in most grocery stores. They are delicious and inexpensive, and I actually prefer them to gluten-free pasta!

SERVES 4:

8.8 oz rice noodles
1 lb beef sirloin
1 serving Barbecue Sauce (see page 160)
Butter for frying
Salt
Pepper

3 carrots
1 scallion, green parts only
1 teaspoon grated fresh ginger
3 eggs
½ teaspoon chili powder
Thyme, or other fresh herbs, to garnish

Soak the rice noodles in lukewarm water for approximately 30 minutes. Slice the beef and mix it with the BBQ sauce. Marinate for a minimum of 30 minutes.

Fry the beef in a little butter, salt, and pepper until medium–well done, and then transfer to a plate. Peel the carrots, wash and slice the scallion, and sauté the vegetables in a little butter for 1–2 minutes. Add the cooked beef, noodles, and grated ginger, and mix well.

Beat the eggs, add them to the noodles, and stir until the eggs are cooked through. Season with salt, pepper, and chili, and any other spice that you can tolerate.

TIPS

You can substitute boiled rice for the rice noodles, and include any vegetable you can tolerate.

You can prepare the beef the day before and marinate it overnight.

CARBONARA NOODLES

This quick and delicious everyday dinner is always a big hit with everyone.

SERVES 3–4:

½ portion Béchamel Sauce (see page 153)

10–14 oz ham cut into small cubes, or bacon, chopped

8.8 oz rice noodles

2 tablespoons grated Parmesan cheese

Make the béchamel sauce and add the ham or bacon. Boil water in a saucepan, add the rice noodles, then remove the saucepan from the heat, and let the noodles soak for 4–5 minutes until they're soft.

Drain and serve the noodles with the sauce and grated Parmesan cheese on top.

TIPS

To make a casserole, put the mixture in an ovenproof dish, sprinkle with cheese, and bake in the oven at 390°F for 10–15 minutes, or until the cheese has melted.

To make crêpes (see page 40), place a little béchamel sauce with ham on each crêpe, roll it up, place it in a baking dish, sprinkle grated cheese on top, and bake at 390°F for about 10 minutes, until the cheese is melted.

OVEN-BAKED COD WITH PESTO AND SERRANO HAM

My mother has the honor of being the one who made this dish come to life. She actually makes a version with monkfish, but cod is another healthy and tasty option.

SERVES 2:

2 6-oz cod or monkfish fillets, or any other white-fleshed fish fillets
1 serving of Basil Pesto (see page 164)

3 ½-5 ½ oz Serrano ham
Freshly ground pepper
Fresh basil, to garnish

Preheat the oven to 400°F. Place the fish in an ovenproof dish. Spread a generous amount of the pesto on top of each fillet and bake on the bottom rack of the oven for about 15 minutes, or until the fish is fully cooked. If the fish is frozen, increase the cooking time to 25-30 minutes.

Chop the Serrano ham and fry it in a skillet over medium heat until crisp.

Place the cooked fish on a plate, top it with the ham, and drizzle over the pesto and juices from the pan. Top with pepper. You do not need additional sauce.

TIPS

Bacon can be substituted for Serrano ham.

This is good when served with boiled new potatoes.

Note: Although Serrano ham is low FODMAP, some people do react to cured meats.

BARBECUE SHRIMP

One of the things I miss most on a low FODMAP diet is garlic marinated shrimp. But with just a small twist, you can make a low FODMAP version!

SERVES 1:

9 oz large shrimp
1 serving Barbecue Sauce (see page 160)
1 teaspoon chili flakes

$3\frac{1}{3}$ tablespoons olive oil
1 teaspoon grated ginger
A pinch of salt

Peel the shrimp, remove the black veins, and pat dry with paper towels. Mix the shrimp with the barbecue sauce and chili flakes, then add the olive oil, grated ginger, and salt. Marinate the shrimp for a few hours in the refrigerator, or overnight.

Preheat the oven to 400°F. Transfer the shrimp to an ovenproof dish and bake on the center rack for approximately 10 minutes.

TIPS

The shrimp can be used for tapas, or as an appetizer, or side dish for 2–3 people.

Cook the shrimp quickly in a grill pan, add cooked rice, mix, and fry it all over high heat. I tasted this dish for the first time in Hawaii, and it has become a household favorite!

CHICKEN CASSEROLE

This one-pot dish is nice and warm on a cold winter day, and best of all it "makes itself" (after you have washed and peeled all the vegetables, that is).

SERVES 4:

5 carrots
1 red bell pepper
1 squash
1 eggplant
½ bunch broccoli
2 scallions, green parts only
10 potatoes
2½ cups canned chopped tomatoes
1 teaspoon grated fresh ginger

1 teaspoon sugar
1 teaspoon oyster sauce
1 tablespoon soy sauce
1 teaspoon salt
½ teaspoon pepper
½ teaspoon cayenne pepper
Approx. 1¾ lbs large chicken pieces
  (with bones)
Fresh thyme, to garnish

Wash and peel the vegetables and cut them into large chunks. Mix all the remaining ingredients together, except the chicken, and put them in the bottom of an ovenproof baking dish.

Rub the chicken pieces with salt and pepper and place them on top of the vegetables. Put the dish in the cold oven on the bottom rack, set the oven temperature to 350°F, and cook for 1 hour and 15 minutes.

TIPS

This chicken casserole also tastes great with rice.

You can use other meats besides chicken. If you use beef, set the oven to 350°F, allow to cook for 2–2½ hours, and the meat will be delicious and tender!

Vary the vegetables according to what you have on hand and what you can tolerate.

WARMING WINTER
BEEF STEW

There's nothing like a hot casserole when it's raining or cold outside!

SERVES 2–3:

1 lb stewing beef
2 tablespoons butter or oil for frying
2 cups grated carrot
1 cup grated fennel
3 carrots, sliced
1¼ cups water

1 tablespoon soy sauce
1 teaspoon paprika
½ teaspoon cayenne pepper
½ teaspoon salt (to taste)
Fresh chopped parsley, to serve
Boiled potatoes, to serve

Cut the beef into 1-inch cubes. Add the butter or oil to a large saucepan and cook the grated carrot and fennel over medium heat for 1–2 minutes. Add the beef, and fry until browned. Pour the water over the meat.

Add the soy sauce, sliced carrots, paprika, cayenne pepper, and salt to the pan. Simmer with the lid on for 2–3 hours.

Taste to adjust seasoning before serving. Sprinkle over parsley and serve with boiled potatoes.

SPICED LAMB CURRY

Indian food is some of the best I know, but most Indian chefs use a lot of onions. Luckily it's possible to make really good homemade curry without them! Some people like and can tolerate very spicy food, while others cannot, so use more or less chili and cayenne pepper depending on your experience.

SERVES 2–3:

Curry spice mix:
4 teaspoons cinnamon
4 teaspoons ground coriander
4 teaspoons ground cumin
4 teaspoons paprika
4 teaspoons turmeric
4 teaspoons ginger
2 teaspoons crushed cloves
4 teaspoons cardamom
4 teaspoons chili powder
4 teaspoons cayenne pepper
3 teaspoons sugar
4 teaspoons salt

3 cups grated carrot
1 lb lamb, cut into 1-inch cubes
2 tablespoons butter or oil for frying
4-5 teaspoons curry spice mix
3 teaspoons tomato purée
2 cups coconut milk
$\frac{1}{4}$ cup water
Boiled rice and fresh chopped cilantro,
   to serve

First make the curry spice mixture. Finely grind all the ingredients together in a spice grinder or food processor. Store in a sealed glass jar. This will make more than you need for the recipe, but it will keep for a few weeks.

Gently fry the carrot and lamb in the butter or oil in a large saucepan, until browned. Add the curry spice mixture and tomato purée and fry for a minute or two more. Add the coconut milk and water, bring to a boil, cover with a lid, and let the curry simmer over low heat for 2–3 hours.

Taste and adjust seasoning before serving with rice and a sprinkling of cilantro.

PORK MEATBALLS IN TOMATO SAUCE

I don't know anyone who doesn't like this dish, but kids especially love it. The pork mixture can be made into burgers and served with Focaccia (see page 92) in place of hamburger buns.

SERVES 3-4:

1 lb pork, preferably a cut with a little fat
1 teaspoon salt
1 teaspoon chili powder
1 teaspoon ginger powder

1 egg, beaten
¼ cup lactose-free cream
Tomato Sauce (see page 158)
Fresh thyme, to garnish

Cut the meat into pieces and mix with the salt and spices. Mix together in a food processor until finely ground. If you have a meat grinder you can use that, of course! Stir in the egg and lactose-free cream.

Fry the meatballs in a skillet over medium heat for 5–6 minutes. Make the tomato sauce, add the meatballs, and simmer for 3–4 minutes.

TIPS

You can substitute ground pork for the meat in the recipe.

Serve the meatballs with rice noodles, rice, or boiled or mashed potatoes.

SAUSAGE STROGANOFF

This dish is very similar to a beef stroganoff, but uses sausages instead.
It makes a rich, robust, and filling meal.

SERVES 3–4:

1 lb sausages (without onion and garlic)
3½ oz tomato purée
1½–2½ cups lactose-free milk
½ teaspoon salt (depending on saltiness
   of the sausages)

½–1 teaspoon cayenne pepper
Fresh rosemary, to garnish

Cut the sausages into small pieces and fry them quickly in a hot skillet. Add
the tomato purée and fry a little more. Add the milk gradually, a little at a time,
stirring constantly until you have a thick tomato sauce.

Season to taste with salt and cayenne pepper, and serve garnished with rosemary.

TIPS

*For a slightly milder sauce you can add ¼ cup
lactose-free cream just before serving.*

*Serve with rice noodles, gluten-free pasta, or rice
for a more substantial dish.*

5

SWEETS

VANILLA BEAN CREAM

This deliciously rich and fragrant vanilla cream is wonderful with desserts.

SERVES 2:

½ cup lactose-free milk
½ teaspoon vanilla sugar or 1 vanilla
   bean
1 tablespoon sugar

1 egg yolk
½ tablespoon cornstarch
½ cup lactose-free cream

Mix the milk, vanilla sugar (or split the vanilla bean down the middle and scrape out the seeds), and sugar in a saucepan and bring to a boil.

In a separate bowl, mix together the egg yolk and cornstarch. Add the hot milk, return the mixture to the saucepan, and heat gently until it has thickened. Do not boil! Let the mixture cool. Whisk the lactose-free cream and mix it into the vanilla cream, a little at a time, adjusting the quantity to taste.

RICE PUDDING

When I was at my worst, rice pudding was the only thing I could eat. Fortunately, it is low FODMAP, as long as you use lactose-free milk and cream.

SERVES 2:

⅔ cup lactose-free cream
1–2 teaspoons vanilla sugar
2–3 tablespoons confectioners' sugar

1⅔ cups ready-made rice pudding made
   with lactose-free milk
Blueberry Compote (see page 128)

Whip the cream, vanilla sugar, and confectioners' sugar together. Gently combine with the rice pudding. If desired, sweeten to taste with more confectioners' sugar and serve with the compote.

BLUEBERRY COMPOTE

Blueberries are extremely soothing for the stomach. I sometimes mix a little of this compote with water for a stomach-calming drink. Note that blueberries are high FODMAP, if you eat more than ⅔ cup.

SERVES 3-4:

2 cups frozen blueberries

⅓–½ cup sugar, to taste

Place the frozen blueberries and sugar in a small saucepan, and bring to a boil. Simmer for a few minutes until thickened and reduced.

STRAWBERRY SORBET

This is a fresh, delicious dessert to enjoy on a hot summer day or to serve with cake, anytime!

SERVES 3–4:

⅓ cup water
½ cup sugar
2 cups strawberries

1 teaspoon vanilla sugar
1 egg white

To make the syrup, boil the water, remove it from the heat, stir in the sugar and let it cool. Hull and roughly chop the strawberries. Place them in a blender with the vanilla sugar, process until combined, and then add in the syrup.

In a separate bowl, whisk the egg white until stiff peaks form. Stir gently into the berry mixture. Freeze using an ice-cream machine, or in the freezer in a shallow container, stirring with a fork every few hours until the sorbet has set.

CRÈME BRÛLÉE

This classic dessert is a winner with dinner guests. Many people think this treat is difficult to make, but it's not hard—just try it!

MAKES 5:

1¼ cups lactose-free cream
3 egg yolks
½ teaspoon vanilla powder

1 tablespoon sugar
Approximately ⅓ cup brown sugar for the topping

Preheat the oven to 300°F. Place the cream in a medium saucepan and bring to a quick boil. Whisk the egg yolks, vanilla powder, and sugar together and pour into the hot cream while continuously stirring.

Pour the mixture into 5 small ovenproof ramekins set in a roasting pan, and pour a little boiling water into the bottom of the roasting pan. Bake the crème brûlées in the oven for 30–40 minutes.

Remove the ramekins from the oven and allow to cool. Sprinkle a thin layer of brown sugar on each custard and melt the sugar with a crème brûlée torch until you have a thin layer of caramelized hard sugar on top. Alternatively, melt the sugar under the broiler. Serve immediately.

TIPS

Add berries to make this dessert even more delicious.

If you do not have vanilla powder, it can be substituted with 1½ teaspoons vanilla sugar. If you do this, only use ½ teaspoon sugar, instead of 1 teaspoon. (Vanilla powder is made from finely ground vanilla beans, while vanilla sugar is flavored with vanilla.)

FRENCH MACARONS

Before I began a low FODMAP diet, I was very fond of macarons and loved making them. Lately, however, I have become very sensitive to almonds, and I needed to find a solution so that I could continue to enjoy my favorite treats. The idea of using finely ground gluten-free oatmeal instead of almond flour came into my head early one morning. Overall, this is the classic French macaron recipe, and it gives the finished macarons a bit more of a chewy consistency, but according to my mother this is a good thing!

MAKES 8–10:

Macarons:
1 egg white
Sugar
Oat flour made from gluten-free
  oatmeal
Confectioners' sugar (see below
  to calculate the dry ingredients)

Filling:
⅔ cup butter
2 ½ tablespoons confectioners' sugar
  (to taste)
8 oz block of Philadelphia cream cheese
⅓ cup white chocolate, melted

Because it is important to use exact ratios when making macarons, weigh the egg white first. Then multiply the egg white weight by 0.8 for the sugar, 1.4 for the oatmeal, and 1.4 for the confectioners' sugar. So, if the egg white weighs 1.2 oz (egg white from one egg often weighs between 1.2-1.4 oz), then you will need 0.96 oz sugar, 1.68 oz oat flour, and 1.68 oz confectioner's sugar.

Place the egg white in a bowl and whisk until stiff peaks form, then add the sugar. Beat for approximately 5 minutes until thick and glossy.

Mix the oat flour and the confectioners' sugar together, and then gently fold into the meringue mixture. Here, it is important that you do not over- or undermix. If you mix too much, the mixture will be very stiff, and if you mix too little, the mixture will become too soft. The consistency is perfect when you can put a spoon of the mixture on parchment paper in a small peak and it is still soft to the touch.

Use two teaspoons to place small peaks of the mixture onto a baking sheet lined with parchment paper. You can also use a piping bag. When the tray is full, tap it firmly on the counter to release any air bubbles. The macarons will then be more stable.

Allow the macarons to rest on the counter for 45 minutes–1 hour so that they can dry out. This will give them a nice outer casing so they won't crack during baking, and they will rise from the bottom and get their distinctive "feet." When the macarons have finished drying, you should be able to touch them lightly without any of the batter sticking to your finger.

Preheat the oven to 300°F. Bake the macarons on the center oven rack for 7–8 minutes. You'll need to watch them carefully, as cooking times can vary from oven to oven. Cool the macarons on the parchment paper before loosening them with a palette knife.

To make the filling, mix the butter and confectioners' sugar together and stir in the cream cheese and chocolate. Spread the filling between two of the macaron halves.

────

TIPS

Making macarons requires a little trial and error. If the macarons don't quite work on the first try, you can break them up and eat them with a mix of yogurt, cream, and berry compote (see page 128), or use them as a low FODMAP addition to a crumble topping, or simply crush them over berries.

If you want to avoid dairy completely, you can substitute baking chocolate that has a minimal amount of powdered milk for the cream cheese and chocolate in the filling.

CHOCOLATE MOUSSE CAKE

Last time I was in France, I bought individual ramekins in the shape of hearts and squares to make my chocolate mousse cakes, but you don't need fancy baking equipment. A round springform pan would work just as well, but you'll need to double the recipe for the crust.

MAKES 1 8-INCH CAKE OR 4 INDIVIDUAL SERVINGS:

Crust:
8½ oz mini gluten-free crackers
2 teaspoons confectioners' sugar
¼ cup butter, melted

Chocolate mousse:
1¼ cup lactose-free cream
3 egg whites
4¼ oz lactose-free cooking chocolate
3 egg yolks

Chocolate topping:
⅓ cup lactose-free cream
3½ oz lactose-free cooking chocolate
Confectioners' sugar, to dust

For the garnish:
Strawberries, sliced

To make a crust for the base of the dessert, crush the crackers and mix them with the confectioners' sugar. Add the melted butter and combine.

To make one large cake, press the crust into the base of an 8-inch cake pan. To make individual servings, press the crust lightly into the bottom of 4 ramekins.

Now begin the mousse by first whipping the cream until stiff. Then, whisk the egg whites until they form stiff peaks. Break up the chocolate and place it in a heatproof container over a saucepan of simmering water. Melt it gently, making sure that the water does not touch the base of the container, and the chocolate stays dry. Whisk the egg yolks lightly and stir them into the lukewarm chocolate. Fold in the egg whites and, finally, the cream. Pour the mousse into the crust, whether making a large cake or individual servings, and chill for 1 hour in the refrigerator.

To make the chocolate topping, warm the ⅓ cup of cream, using the same double boiler method as for the chocolate. Remove the pan from the burner and stir in the 3 ½ oz of chocolate. When the mixture is at room temperature, pour it over the mousse. Let it chill in the refrigerator for 2–3 hours.

Dust with confectioners' sugar, garnish with fresh, sliced strawberries and serve.

CHOCOLATE DREAM CAKE

"Can you make the good chocolate cake?" is a question I often get asked by friends and family. This is the recipe they're talking about. It's a hit with most people!

Cake:
2 eggs
¾ cup sugar
1 cup all-purpose gluten-free flour
2 tablespoons cocoa powder
1 teaspoon baking powder
⅔ cup oil or butter, melted
½ cup coconut milk or lactose-free cream

Chocolate topping:
½ cup lactose-free cream
3 ½ oz lactose-free cooking chocolate

Preheat the oven to 350°F. Beat the eggs and sugar together until smooth. In a separate bowl, sift the flour, cocoa, and the baking powder. Add the flour to the egg mixture and stir in the melted butter, or oil, and coconut milk or cream.

Grease a 10-inch springform cake pan with butter, and pour in the batter. Bake the cake for 20–25 minutes on the center rack. Let cool completely.

To make the chocolate topping, first place the cream in a small saucepan and warm over low heat. Remove it from the heat and stir in the chocolate until it's completely melted. Occasionally stir the chocolate mix, while waiting for it to cool to room temperature.

When the topping has reached room temperature, gently pour it over the cake, while the cake is still in the pan. Let the cake cool for an hour before removing it from the pan.

—
TIP

Serve with a dollop of lactose-free cream and a cup of coffee, if you can tolerate it: this is a real "coffee cake."

INDIVIDUAL CHOCOLATE CAKES

The good thing about both lactose-free cream and pre-made gluten-free muffins is that they have long shelf lives. I always have some in the house, so I always have what I need to make a quick and easy base for small cream cakes.

Gluten-free muffins (one per person)
Lactose-free milk, for dipping
Jam and Vanilla Bean Cream (see page 126) or lactose-free whipped cream

Chocolate cream:
1¼ cups lactose-free cream
1 cup confectioners' sugar
1–1½ tablespoons cocoa powder

Slice each muffin in half. Pour the milk into a bowl. Quickly dip the muffins into the milk and then drain them on a paper towel. Spread the cut halves with jam and vanilla cream, or whipped cream, and sandwich together. Then put some extra cream on top!

This chocolate cream is so good, and it's almost embarrassing to say how easy it is to make. Mix the cream, sugar, and cocoa together and whip until creamy.

TIP

The chocolate cream can be used both on cakes and muffins, and is delicious with strawberries.

LEMON MUFFINS

You can call these little treats cupcakes or muffins—they are delicious either way!

MAKES 12 SMALL CAKES:

½ cup butter
¾ cup sugar
2 eggs
¼ cup lactose-free plain or vanilla
    yogurt
¼ cup lactose-free cream
4 teaspoons lemon juice
Zest of 1 lemon

1¼ cups all-purpose gluten-free flour
1 teaspoon baking powder

Buttercream frosting:
½ cup butter
½ cup confectioners' sugar
2 teaspoons lemon juice

Preheat the oven to 360°F. Whisk the butter and sugar together until well combined. Add the eggs one by one, whisking them well to combine. Mix the yogurt, cream, lemon juice, and lemon zest, and add them to the butter, sugar, and egg mixture. Sift the flour and baking powder into the batter, and stir until combined.

Pour the batter into muffin molds and bake on the center rack of the oven for 15–20 minutes.

For the frosting, beat the butter, sugar, and lemon juice into a creamy mixture. If the topping looks too thin, add a little more sugar. You can frost the muffins with a piping bag, or use a palette knife to spread the buttercream.

TIPS

Orange juice can be substituted for the lemon juice.

If you want to take these muffins on a trip, use the buttercream as a filling instead of frosting. Simply slice each muffin in half and fill. They will keep for 3–4 days in a sealed container.

CARROT CAKE CUPCAKES

The first time I tasted carrot cake was 20 years ago, when I was in school. This cake quickly became a favorite—it's easy to make, tastes heavenly, and is of course low FODMAP. In this recipe, I've made the cake into cupcakes.

MAKES 10–12 MUFFINS:

2 eggs
1¼ cups sugar
½ cups all-purpose gluten-free flour
½ teaspoon baking soda (if your flour does not contain baking soda already, increase the quantity to 1 teaspoon)
1½ teaspoons cinnamon
⅓ oil
¾ cup grated carrot

Cream cheese frosting:
⅓ cup butter
¼ cup lactose-free cream cheese
¼ cup confectioners' sugar

Preheat the oven to 350°F.

Beat the eggs and sugar together and stir in the flour, baking soda, and cinnamon. Add the oil and carrots and mix well. Let the batter rest for 5–10 minutes before scooping into muffin cups.

Bake the cupcakes for 10–13 minutes on the center rack of the oven.

For the cream cheese frosting, beat the butter, cream cheese, and sugar together until creamy, then spread or pipe it onto the cooled cupcakes.

TIPS

If you want to avoid dairy altogether, you can leave out the cream cheese and make a frosting with dairy-free butter and sugar.

If you want to make a cake instead of cupcakes, double the recipe and bake the cake in a 10-inch springform pan for 25–30 minutes at 350°F.

OAT BUTTER COOKIES

While these cookies are not exactly healthy, they are more filling and satisfying than regular cookies, because of the oat flour. They are thin and crispy, and make a great treat.

MAKES 9 COOKIES:

¼ cup butter
¼ cup sugar
¼ cup oat flour

1 tablespoon all-purpose gluten-free flour
½ teaspoon baking soda

Preheat the oven to 350°F. Melt the butter and mix in all the other ingredients. Line a baking sheet with parchment paper and drop the cookie batter onto the sheet in spoonfuls. Remember that the cookies will spread as they cook, so leave space between them.

Bake the cookies on the center rack of the oven for 6–7 minutes. Watch the cookies carefully towards the end of the baking time, as they will suddenly be done!

TIP

If you are following a low FODMAP diet and do not have celiac disease, you can use regular oats (see page 14).

CHOCOLATE–COVERED STRAWBERRIES AND CREAM

The acidity of the strawberries, along with the sweetness of the chocolate, make this dessert absolutely perfect!

SERVES 3–4:

2 cups whole, fresh strawberries

1 cup vegetable shortening

1 cup lactose-free cooking chocolate

1¼ cups lactose-free cream, to serve

Rinse the strawberries, but leave the stems on. Dry the strawberries well.

Place the vegetable shortening in a small saucepan and melt it over low heat. Remove the pan from the heat and add the chocolate. It is important not to melt the chocolate over the heat, or it may turn grainy. Stir until the chocolate has melted into the shortening and continue to stir occasionally, while allowing the mixture to cool to room temperature. When the chocolate has cooled sufficiently, the mixture will thicken.

Dip the strawberries one by one into the chocolate and place the berries on a baking sheet lined with waxed paper. Place them in the refrigerator to set.

Serve with whipped lactose-free cream.

TIPS

These strawberries are great as cake decorations, or as a decadent treat with a glass of champagne.

Although strawberries are low FODMAP, some people react to the acid in the berries. Find out how much you can tolerate.

CARAMEL CAKE WITH OAT TOPPING

This cake might not look very refined, but it is delicious, especially with a little lactose-free whipped cream!

Cake:
⅔ cup butter, plus 1 tablespoon
2 eggs
¾ cup sugar
1 cup all-purpose gluten-free flour
½ teaspoon baking powder
⅓ cup lactose-free cream

Topping:
⅓ cup butter
¾ cup sugar
1¼ tablespoons gluten-free flour
1¼ tablespoons lactose-free milk
⅓ cup oats

Preheat the oven to 350°F.

Melt the butter. Beat the eggs and sugar together in a bowl. Sift in the flour with the baking powder and stir to combine. Add the butter and cream to the bowl, then mix until smooth. Grease a 10-inch cake pan with butter and pour the batter into the pan. Bake the cake for 20 minutes on the bottom rack of the oven.

To make the topping, mix all the ingredients in a medium saucepan and gently warm the mixture. Do not allow it to boil. Pour the topping onto the cake after 20 minutes of baking time. It doesn't matter if the topping is not evenly distributed, as it will spread out over the cake when it goes back in the oven. Return the cake to the oven for approximately 15 more minutes, or until the topping has melted.

TIPS

If you can tolerate almonds, use approximately 6 tablespoons chopped almonds in the topping instead of oats.

The cake can be made in a loaf pan, without the topping.

BLUEBERRY CRUMBLE

My husband claims he could eat this low FODMAP blueberry crumble every single day—and he is not even particularly fond of cakes and desserts! Blueberries are low FODMAP, if you do not eat more than ½ cup.

MAKES I LARGE PIE:

Crumble dough:
½ cup sugar
1¾ cups all-purpose gluten-free flour
½ cup butter
6 tablespoons lactose-free cream

Filling:
2 cups fresh or frozen blueberries
1½ teaspoons sugar

Preheat the oven to 400°F.

Mix the sugar and flour together in a bowl. Chop the butter into the flour and add the cream. Stir lightly, then, using your fingertips, rub the dough until it resembles rough breadcrumbs. The dough should be grainy, but combined.

Sprinkle a layer, approximately half of the crumble mixture, into the bottom of an 8-inch pan. Spoon the blueberries into the pie pan and sprinkle with the sugar. Spread the remaining crumble dough on top of the blueberries and bake on the center rack of the oven for 30–40 minutes.

TIPS

The crumble can be made the day before. Reheat it in the oven at 300°F for approximately 10 minutes.

Serve with lactose-free ice cream, lactose-free whipped cream mixed with some vanilla sugar, or Vanilla Bean Cream (see page 126).

You can also make this crumble with other berries or fruits that you like and can tolerate.

SAUCES & SEASONINGS

CREAM SAUCE

Some people on a gluten-free diet use cornstarch to thicken sauces, but I prefer rice flour. It gives the sauce a consistency similar to sauces that use wheat flour.

SERVES 2–3:

¼ cup butter

2 tablespoons rice flour
2 cups lactose-free milk
Salt

Melt the butter in a small saucepan over medium heat and add the rice flour. Whisk continuously, while adding the milk. Allow the sauce to simmer for 10 minutes, whisking continuously. If the sauce is too thick, add a little more milk. Season with salt to taste.

MUSTARD SAUCE

This sauce is delicious with chicken and fish.

SERVES 2–3:

Cream Sauce (see above), but made
   with 2 ½ cups lactose-free milk
1½ tablespoons whole-grain mustard

3-4 tablespoons finely chopped parsley
1 tablespoon white wine vinegar

Make the cream sauce as above. Add the mustard, chopped parsley, and vinegar and simmer gently for 1 minute. Remove from the heat and serve.

BÉCHAMEL SAUCE

This is a relatively thick, white cheese sauce that can be used for lasagna, pasta carbonara, or fish.

SERVES 2–3:

⅓ cup butter
¼ cup rice flour

3⅓–3⅔ cups lactose-free milk
3½ oz Gouda or Jarlsberg cheese, grated
Salt and pepper

Melt the butter in a saucepan over medium heat. Add the rice flour, while whisking continuously.

Pour 3 ⅓ cups milk into the mixture gradually, stirring constantly, and bring to a boil. Rice flour takes a little longer to thicken than plain wheat flour, so allow the sauce to cook over low heat for 10-12 minutes, whisking continuously.

If the sauce becomes too thick, add a little more milk. Then add the cheese and heat until the cheese melts. Season to taste with salt and pepper.

CREAMY KETCHUP

This tangy sauce is great with fish dishes.

SERVES 2–3:

Cream Sauce (see opposite)

1 tablespoon ketchup

Make the cream sauce as directed, and then mix in the ketchup.

BROWN SAUCE

This sauce, shown opposite, is delicious with cold cuts and meatballs.

SERVES 3–4:

1¼ tablespoons butter
2 tablespoons rice flour
2½ cups water, stock or bouillon
   (without onion)

Drops of caramel food coloring
Lactose-free cream (optional)
Pinch of pepper
Pinch of cayenne pepper
Pinch of salt

Melt the butter in a saucepan over medium heat. Mix in the flour and stir until the flour browns a little. Add the water, stock, or bouillon and bring to a boil while constantly stirring. Add a few drops of food coloring, and let the mixture simmer for 5–10 minutes. Remove the pan from the heat, add a little cream, if desired, then season with pepper, cayenne pepper, and salt.

If you used water or a stock with a mild flavor, you can add a little extra salt. If the sauce is too thick, add some water. If the sauce is too thin, stir some rice flour into a little water and pour the mixture into the sauce, while whisking continuously (do not let the sauce boil as you add in the flour mixture).

RED WINE SAUCE

Red wine sauce without onions sounds a bit pitiful, but I promise you that this sauce is deliciously flavorful. It is excellent with steaks and other beef dishes.

SERVES 2–3:

1 carrot
2 scallions, green parts only
1 tablespoon butter
1 teaspoon tomato purée
2 teaspoons Balsamic Glaze (see
  page 164)

1 sprig fresh thyme
¾ cup red wine
¾ cup stock or bouillon
  (without onion)
Salt
Pepper
A pinch of sugar

Peel and chop the carrots, chop the green parts of the scallions, and sauté in butter in a saucepan for approximately 1 minute. Add the tomato purée, balsamic glaze, and thyme and stir. Add the red wine, constantly stirring, and finally add the stock or bouillon. Bring to a boil and simmer for 5–10 minutes. Strain the sauce into a bowl.

Put the sauce back into the pan and cook over medium heat (allow the liquid to evaporate a bit), stirring, until it thickens. Season with salt and pepper, taste, and add a pinch of sugar if necessary. (As there is sugar in the balsamic glaze, you may not need it.)

TIP

If you are in a hurry, you can thicken the sauce with 1 teaspoon of rice flour, mixed with some water, instead of cooking the sauce for a second time. Remove the saucepan from the heat and pour the rice flour mixture into the sauce, while constantly stirring. Simmer the sauce for 5 minutes, stirring.

TOMATO SAUCE

This tomato sauce goes extremely well with ground beef in bolognese and chili con carne recipes, and is also perfect for pizza and pasta!

SERVES 3-4:

1 tablespoon oil
2 carrots, grated
2 tablespoons tomato purée
2 ½ cups canned chopped tomatoes
1-2 tablespoons dried herbs, such as oregano, thyme, rosemary, basil
½ teaspoon sugar

1 teaspoon Balsamic Glaze (see page 164) or ½ teaspoon balsamic or white wine vinegar mixed with ½ teaspoon sugar
Salt and pepper
Pinch chili powder
Fresh thyme, or other fresh herbs, to garnish

Heat the oil in a saucepan and cook the grated carrots for 2-3 minutes over medium heat. Add the tomato purée and chopped tomatoes, and simmer for a couple of minutes before tasting.

Season with the the herbs, sugar, balsamic glaze, salt, pepper, and chili powder, and simmer for 10 minutes more.

——

TIP

The carrots add texture to this sauce, so you can decide how much you want to use.

BARBECUE SAUCE

Yes, you can make your own barbecue sauce without onion and garlic—and it is really good! I use this sauce for red meat, chicken, and shrimp.

SERVES 2–3:

½ cup ketchup
3 tablespoons Balsamic Glaze (see page 164)
3 tablespoons olive oil
3 teaspoons soy sauce
3 teaspoons salt
1 teaspoon pepper

1 teaspoon chili powder or crushed red chili pepper (I prefer the latter because it provides a nice texture)
1 teaspoon cayenne pepper
1 teaspoon ginger
1 tsp sesame oil

I use balsamic glaze rather than balsamic vinegar in this recipe because I want the thickness, acid, and sweetness from the glaze. When it comes to salt, pepper, and other spice, add as much as you want. Paprika, chives, rosemary, curry powder, cumin, oregano, and thyme are just a few of the spices and herbs you can use, as well as, or instead of, the ones I've mentioned here. Just add your favorites and taste the sauce as you go.

Mix all the ingredients together in a bowl. Use immediately or store in a glass container with a lid. The sauce will keep well for 1–2 weeks in the refrigerator.

TIPS

Use garlic-infused oil (see page 17) instead of the olive oil. Garlic-infused oil contains all of the flavor of garlic and none of the fructans.

You can customize this sauce with any fresh herbs you have available. Add 1 teaspoon chopped rosemary, 1 tablespoon chopped oregano, and 1 tablespoon chopped thyme for an Italian flavor.

MAYONNAISE

When dining out, I avoid food with sauce because I'm so afraid of onions and garlic. At home, however, it is easy to make good sauces and dressings without garlic, such as this creamy mayonnaise.

SERVES 2:

1 egg yolk
½ teaspoon mustard or 1 teaspoon
white wine vinegar

Pinch of salt and white pepper
Approx. ¼ teaspoon sugar
4 tablespoons corn or sunflower oil
4 tablespoons olive oil

Whisk the egg yolk, mustard or vinegar, salt, pepper, and sugar together in a bowl. Add the oil, little by little, in a steady, thin stream, whisking continuously. It is important that you continue whisking until the mayonnaise has emulsified and is thick and creamy.

TIPS

You can use any neutral-tasting oil you prefer— sunflower, corn, or canola oil will all work and can replace the olive oil.

The acid in the mustard or vinegar brings out the flavor in the mayonnaise and prevents it from becoming too cloying. You can substitute lemon juice, if you like.

If you want to make an aioli-like mayonnaise, add some finely chopped scallions (green parts only) or chives.

Make a remoulade: add approximately 3 tablespoons of finely chopped pickles and some white pepper.

SOUR CREAM DRESSING

I love salad, but only if I can drizzle a delicious dressing all over it! Use this recipe as a base that can be flavored with whatever spices you like and can tolerate. This dressing is great for both salads and dips.

SERVES 2:

¾ cup lactose-free sour cream
Approx. 3–3½ tablespoons ketchup
1 teaspoon Balsamic Glaze (see page 164)

½ cup cottage cheese (if omitted, use a little less ketchup)
Pinch of salt, pepper, or cayenne pepper, or chili powder

Mix the sour cream with the rest of the ingredients. If you are adding cottage cheese to the dressing, use a hand blender to make it smooth and lump-free.

Note: There are .05 oz of lactose per 3.5 oz of cottage cheese. That is a very small amount, considering that you will not eat more than ¼ of the dressing this recipe makes. Most people will be able to tolerate that amount of lactose.

———
TIP

Other flavoring ideas include curry powder, oregano, and paprika. Use your favorite herbs and spices.

BASIL PESTO

Pesto goes with everything and can be served with pasta, or as a dip for bread. It can also be used instead of butter in sandwiches, or as a dressing. If you can't tolerate the green parts of scallions or leeks, omit them.

SERVES 2:

½ tablespoon pine nuts
2 tablespoons fresh basil

⅓ cup olive oil
Chopped leeks or scallions (green parts only), or chives
2 tablespoons grated Parmesan cheese

Place the pine nuts and basil in a blender with the oil and process to combine. Add the leeks, scallions, or chives, and process for a few seconds more. Stir in the grated Parmesan.

BALSAMIC GLAZE

This thick balsamic glaze has so much more flavor than ordinary balsamic vinegar, and is so simple to make.

SERVES 2:

½ cup balsamic vinegar
1-1 ½ tablespoons brown sugar
Pinch of salt

Stir the balsamic vinegar, sugar, and salt together in a non-stick skillet over medium–high heat. Bring the mixture to a boil while stirring constantly. Reduce the heat to a simmer and stir constantly for 10–15 minutes, until the vinegar is reduced by about half. Make sure it doesn't burn! Cool and store the glaze in a lidded glass container or jar.

CREAMY HERB SALAD DRESSING

This very simple, but delicious, recipe is an excellent alternative to Ranch or Caesar salad dressings!

SERVES 1:

1 tablespoon lactose-free sour cream
1 tablespoon Balsamic Glaze (see opposite)
4 tablespoons olive oil
Pinch of grated ginger

Salt
Pepper
Chili powder
Dried basil or Herbes de Provence
A little grated Parmesan

Mix the sour cream and balsamic glaze together in a small bowl. Add the olive oil, stirring continuously. Stir in the rest of the ingredients and taste to adjust seasoning.

TIP

If you do not have lactose-free sour cream, or you want the dressing to be completely dairy-free, you can make it as a simple oil dressing, i.e., without the sour cream.

LOW FODMAP FOODS

The foods listed below are low in Fermentable Oligosaccharides, Disaccharides, Monosaccharides, and Polyols, and are therefore unlikely to cause gut problems.
For up-to-date lists, as well as resources, FAQs, and the latest research, visit the Monash University FODMAP website at http://www.med.monash.edu/cecs/gastro/fodmap/low-high.html

VEGETABLES AND LEGUMES

Alfalfa
Bamboo shoots
Bean sprouts
Bok choy
Broccoli—½ cup
Brussels sprouts—1 serving of 2 sprouts
Butternut squash—¼ cup
Cabbage, common and red—up to 1 cup
Callaloo
Carrots
Celery root
Celery—less than 2-inch stalk
Chard
Chayote
Chicory leaves
Chickpeas—¼ cup
Chili powder / chili peppers—if tolerable
Chives
Choy sum
Collard greens
Corn—only in small amounts—½ cob
Cucumber
Eggplant
Fennel
Green beans
Green bell pepper
Ginger
Kale
Leeks (green part)

Lentils—in small amounts
Lettuce:
   Arugula
   Butter lettuce
   Iceberg lettuce
   Radicchio
   Red Coral lettuce
Okra
Olives
Parsnip
Peas, snow—5 pods
Pickled gherkins
Potato
Pumpkin
Pumpkin, canned—¼ cup, 2.2 oz
Radish
Red bell pepper
Scallions (green part)
Seaweed
Spaghetti squash
Spinach, baby
Squash
Sun-dried tomatoes—4 pieces
Swiss chard
Sweet potato—½ cup
Tomato—canned, cherry, common, Roma
Turnip
Water chestnuts
Yam
Zucchini

FRUIT
Ackee
Bananas
Blueberries
Breadfruit
Carambola
Cantaloupe
Cranberry
Clementine
Dragon fruit
Grapes
Guava, ripe
Honeydew and Galia melons
Kiwifruit
Lemon, including lemon juice
Lime, including lime juice
Oranges, including Mandarin
Passion fruit
Papaya
Pineapple
Plantain, peeled
Raspberry
Rhubarb
Rutabaga
Strawberry
Tamarind
Tangelo

MEATS, POULTRY, AND MEAT SUBSTITUTES
Beef
Chicken
Lamb
Pork
Prosciutto
Serrano ham
Turkey
Cold cuts, such as other hams and
turkey breast

FISH AND SEAFOOD
Canned tuna

Fresh fish e.g.
  Cod
  Haddock
  Plaice
  Salmon
  Trout
  Tuna

Seafood
  Crab
  Lobster
  Mussels
  Oysters
  Shrimp

CEREALS, GRAINS, BREADS, PASTA, AND NUTS
Cereals:
  Buckwheat
  Buckwheat flour
  Buckwheat noodles
  Cornflakes—½ cup
  Oatmeal—½ cup
  Oats and oat-based cereals

Grains:
  Bulgur—¼ cup cooked
  Brown rice / whole-grain rice
  Millet
  Polenta
  Popcorn
  Quinoa
  Sorghum
  Tortilla chips / corn chips

Bread:

Bread, wheat—1 slice

Corn bread

Corn cakes

Corn tortillas—3 tortillas

Crackers, plain

Gluten-free breads

Oat bread

Oatcakes

Potato flour bread

Pretzels

Rice bread

Spelt sourdough bread

Wheat-free breads

Pasta:

Pasta, wheat—up to ½ cup cooked

Wheat-free or gluten-free pasta

Nuts:

Almonds—max of 15

Brazil nuts

Chestnuts

Coconut—milk, cream, flesh

Hazelnuts—max of 15

Macadamia nuts

Mixed nuts

Peanuts

Pecans—max of 15

Pine nuts—max of 15

Walnuts

Rice:

Basmati rice

Brown rice

Rice noodles

Rice bran

Rice cakes

Rice crackers

Rice flakes

Rice flour

Rice Krispies®

White rice

Seeds:

Chia seeds

Poppy seeds

Pumpkin seeds

Sesame seeds

Sunflower seeds

CONDIMENTS, SWEETS, SWEETENERS, AND SPREADS

Condiments:

Apple cider vinegar—2 tablespoons

Balsamic vinegar—2 tablespoons

Barbecue sauce

Capers in vinegar

Capers, salted

Chutney—1 tablespoon

Fish sauce

Garlic-infused oil

Ketchup—less than 1 tablespoon

Mayonnaise—without garlic or onion
  in ingredients

Miso paste

Mustard

Oyster sauce

Pesto—less than 1 tablespoon

Rice wine vinegar

Shrimp paste

Soy sauce

Sweet and sour sauce

Tamarind paste

Wasabi

Worcestershire sauce

Sweets:

Dark chocolate

Milk chocolate—3 squares

White chocolate—3 squares

Sweeteners:
- Acesulfame K
- Aspartame
- Glucose syrup
- Golden syrup
- Maple syrup
- Rice malt syrup
- Saccharine
- Stevia
- Sucralose
- Sugar—sucrose

Spreads:
- Jam / jelly, strawberry
- Marmalade
- Peanut butter

DRINKS AND PROTEIN POWDERS

Alcohol—is an irritant to the gut, limited intake advised:
- Beer—limited to one drink
- Clear spirits such as vodka and gin —limited to 1 serving (1 oz)
- Whiskey—limited to 1 serving (1 oz)
- Wine—limited to one drink

Coffee:
- Espresso coffee, regular or decaffeinated, black espresso coffee, regular or decaffeinated, with up to 1 cup lactose-free milk
- Espresso, regular, black
- Instant coffee, regular or decaffeinated, black, with up to 1 cup lactose-free milk

Protein powders:
- Egg protein
- Pea protein— up to ¼ cup
- Rice protein

- Sacha Inchi protein
- Whey protein isolate
- Soy milk made with soy protein

Soft Drinks:
- Drinking chocolate powder
- Fruit juice—½ cup and safe fruits only
- Lemonade—in low quantities
- Malted chocolate powder—3 teaspoon
- Sugar-free soft drinks, in low quantities, as aspartame and acesulfame can be irritants
- Sugary soft drinks that do not contain high fructose corn syrup, such as lemonade, and colas. Limit intake, as these drinks are generally unhealthy and possibly cause gut irritation

Tea:
- Black tea, weak
- Chai tea, weak
- Fruit and herbal tea, weak—no apple added
- Green tea
- Peppermint tea
- White tea

DAIRY FOODS AND EGGS

Butter

Cheese:
- Brie
- Camembert
- Cheddar
- Cottage Cheese
- Feta
- Goat / chevre
- Mozzarella
- Parmesan
- Ricotta—2 tablespoons
- Swiss

Cream—½ cup

Lactose-free chocolate pudding

Eggs

Margarine

Milk:

    Almond milk

    Hemp milk

    Lactose-free milk

    Oat milk—2 tablespoons

    Soy milk

    Rice milk—up to ¾ cup

Sorbet

Soy protein (avoid soy beans)

Tempeh (which is low FODMAP despite
being made from soy beans)

Tofu—drained and firm varieties (not
silken)

Whipped cream

Yogurt, lactose-free

Yogurt, Greek, in small amounts

Yogurt, goat

COOKING AND BAKING INGREDIENTS, HERBS, AND SPICES

Asafetida powder—great onion substitute

Baking powder

Baking soda

Cacao powder

Cocoa powder

Confectioners' sugar

Gelatin

Ghee

Lard

Salt

Herbs:

Basil, cilantro, curry leaves,
fenugreek, lemongrass, mint, oregano, parsley,
rosemary, tarragon, thyme

Spices:

Allspice, black pepper, cardamom,
chili powder (check ingredients, sometimes
contains garlic), cinnamon, cloves, cumin,
curry powder, fennel seeds, five spice,
mustard seeds, nutmeg, paprika, saffron, star
anise, turmeric

Oils:

avocado oil, canola oil, coconut oil,
olive oil, peanut oil, rice bran oil, sesame oil,
sunflower oil, vegetable oil

RESOURCES

FURTHER READING

The Academy of Nutrition and Dietetics
www.eatright.org
Information about IBS and other digestive disorders, as well as a database of Registered Dietitian Nutritionists (RDNs) in the USA.

The American Gastroenterological Association
www.gastro.org/patient-care/conditions-diseases/irritable-bowel-syndrome
Resources about IBS symptoms and treatments, including an online community.

The Complete Low FODMAP Diet: The Revolutionary Plan for Managing IBS and Other Digestive Disorders – Dr. Sue Shepherd, PhD and Dr. Peter Gibson, MD (Penguin Group Australia, 2011)

The International Foundation for Functional Gastrointestinal Disorders
www.aboutibs.org
A nonprofit organization offering knowledge, support, and assistance for those with IBS.

Monash University
www.med.monash.edu/cecs/gastro/fodmap/
Resources to support a low FODMAP diet, including lists of low and high FODMAP foods and details of the Monash FODMAP mobile app for iPhone and Android.

Monash University Low FODMAP Diet blog *www.fodmapmonash.blogspot.co.uk*

ALLERGY CARDS
These cards are available in a variety of languages, with custom text to suit your allergies or dietary requirements. They are an easy way to communicate your needs when traveling, even if you do not speak the language.

Select Wisely
www.selectwisely.com
Several websites (such as Select Wisely), offer a selection of allergy cards, translation cards and emergency cards.

SafeFARE
www.safefare.org
Free PDF templates that you can download and fill in with your own dietary information, in Chinese, Dutch, French, German, Italian, Japanese, Portuguese, Spanish, and Swedish.

INDEX

About the Author

A native of Bergen, Norway, Cecilie Hauge Ågotnes discovered the Low FODMAP programme developed at Monash University in Melbourne, Australia, after suffering from IBS and other chronic illnesses. She has documented her developing understanding of her condition via her blog at www.lowfodmapblog. com and regularly speaks at conferences and to hospital patient groups on the low FODMAP diet and mastering IBS. As a fantastic home cook, she has develops original recipes that taste delicious yet are on the lowest FODMAP rating.

Thank you!

The team at Elwin Street Productions: without you, there wouldn't have been an English translation, thank you! Frode, my editor in Vigmostad & Bjørke: thank you for always being there for me! My former Norwegian publisher Aschehoug: thank you for believing in me and this book!

Christin: this book would not have been the same without your photography. Thank you for a fabulous collaboration, lots of laughter, and amazing pictures.

Janne-Celin, from Janne-Celin Makeup and Styling: thank you for helping me with my makeup and styling. To get dressed up and dolled up with you was a new experience and I'd love to do it again! Erik, from Glass Thomsen: thank you for letting me, without hesitation, borrow the pots and pans for the pictures. Nordnes Verksteder: thank you for your first interest in producing low FODMAP books. I look forward to a continued cooperation. My good friend and model in the book, Elisabet from Kolbrun Retorikk: thank you for good conversations, help with both pictures and text, and your eternal optimism.

Siv Unni, Tone Yvonne and Hege—the best friends in the world!
What would I do without you?

Mum and Dad and my big brothers, Lars-Erik and Harald: I would not be who I am today without you! Joachim, the best son in the world: thank you for your opinions, and for always being honest and interested in your mother's many projects.

Last but not least, Thomas, my husband, and my dearest and best friend since we were 16 years old: thank you for always believing in me and supporting me through thick and thin. I love you.

Other friends and family: a thousand thanks. Everyone should have cheerleaders like you!